Salads

SALADS

Editorial Director
  DONALD D. WOLF

Design and Layout
  MARGOT L. WOLF

Published by
LEXICON PUBLICATIONS, INC.
387 Park Avenue South, New York, NY 10016

Cover illustration:
Mixed Salad with
Blue Cheese Sour Cream Dressing

Opposite title page:
Shrimp and Avocado Salad

Copyright © 1986 by
Advance Publishers
1146 Solana Avenue
Winter Park, Florida 32789

ISBN: 0-7172-4516-0

Contents

Introduction

Salads bring to the table an ineffable touch of freshness. Composed of fresh or cooked foods, touched to piquancy by the right dressing and usually accompanied by a flash of green, they appeal to eye and taste and satisfy both. Today's salad recipes, conspicuously missing from cookbooks 50 years ago, show a riot of inventiveness in creating new combinations of ingredients for interesting and tantalizing results.

Salads are exciting! Look at the variety – salads made with fruits, vegetables and hearty protein foods; salads tossed, molded or frozen; salads for appetizer, main course, accompaniment or dessert.

Salads are worthwhile eating! Look at the appetite appeal of these health-giving foods – fresh vegetables and fruits chock-full of needed vitamins and minerals; protein-rich meat and fish, poultry, cheese and eggs; salad greens and raw vegetables for bulk, necessary for good digestion.

A salad is only as good as its makings so select the ingredients with care. Greens should be fresh, crisp and dry, vegetables garden-fresh, and fruits firm, fully ripe and free from blemish. When using canned products choose those of good quality and appearance. Meat, poultry, fish, cheese and eggs should be fresh. Use only the appetizing leftovers.

A salad should have a carefree look, not too carefully arranged to look overhandled nor too carelessly prepared to look untidy. A salad should fit the serving dish, not skimpily nor too full.

A salad is complemented by the dressing so suit it to the salad. Dressings should coat the greens, not drown them; they should accompany the salad, not hide it.

GELATIN TECHNIQUES – Recipes will remind you:
Lightly oil molds with a flavorless salad or cooking oil (not olive oil). Invert mold to drain excess oil.
Rinse molds with cold water when shiny coating of oil is not desirable; invert to drain.
Soften gelatin in liquid as specified in recipes.
Dissolve softened gelatin *completely* as recipe directs, over very hot water or in very hot liquid.
Chill gelatin mixtures in the refrigerator, stirring occasionally, or over ice and water, stirring frequently, until of desired consistency. Chill gelatin mixtures until slightly thicker than consistency of thick, unbeaten egg white before adding remainder of ingredients, such as chopped or whole foods which would sink to bottom of mold if the gelatin were not sufficiently thickened. When gelatin mixture is already thick because of ingredients or is not a clear mixture, chill until it begins to gel (gets slightly thicker) before adding chopped or whole foods.
Prevent separation of layered molds by chilling gelatin mixtures until slightly set (each mixture is of same consistency); layers should be of almost same consistency when turning one mixture onto another so that they will be fused when unmolded.
Unmold gelatin by running tip of knife around edge of mold to loosen and to permit air to get into mold. Invert mold onto chilled serving plate. If mold does not loosen because of air lock, wet a clean towel in hot water and wring almost dry. Wrap hot towel around mold for a few seconds only. If mold still does not loosen, repeat.
Beat whipping cream to a medium consistency (piles softly), not soft peaks, when it is to be blended with a gelatin mixture.

SALAD GREENS AND PREPARATION – The many kinds of greens star in the tossed salad and form the background of other salads. Select greens that are fresh, blemish-free and firm. In general, wash before storing, drain thoroughly and gently pat dry with a soft, clean towel or absorbent paper. Place in the refrigerator in vegetable drawers or plastic bags, or wrap tightly in waxed paper, moisture-vapor-proof material or aluminum foil to prevent greens from wilting, unless refrigerator maintains a comparatively high humidity.

Never soak greens when washing them. If necessary, crisp them by placing them for a short time in ice and water. Before using, remove every bit of moisture left from washing or crisping.
Lettuce – Discard bruised and wilted leaves; rinse; drain; dry. *Cups* – Remove core from head lettuce with sharp, pointed knife; let cold water run into core cavity to loosen leaves; drain; gently pull leaves from head; cut off heavy, coarse ends; pat dry. *Head* or *Iceberg* – firm, compact head of medium-green outside leaf, pale green heart. *Butterhead* or *Boston* – soft, lighter head of light green outside leaf, light yellow heart; not as crisp as ice-

berg. *Romaine* or *Cos* – green elongated head with coarser leaf and stronger flavor than iceberg. *Bibb* or *Limestone* – head similar to Boston in size and shape; deep green leaves with delicate flavor. *Leaf* – many varieties grown commercially and in the home garden; leafy bunches of curly-edged leaves.

Cabbage – Store in cool place without washing. Discard bruised and wilted outside leaves, rinse, cut into quarters and remove core; chop or shred as directed in recipes. *Early* or *new* – pointed heads. *Danish-type* – staple winter cabbage; compact head. *Savoy* – round head of yellowish, crimped leaves. *Celery* or *Chinese* – long, oval-shaped head of pale green to white leaves; characteristics of romaine and cabbage. *Red* – very tight head of purple leaves.

Endive – Discard bruised and wilted leaves; rinse; drain; dry. *Curly endive* (often called chicory) – bunchy head with narrow, ragged-edged curly leaves; dark green outside, pale yellow heart; pleasant bitter taste. *Broad-leaf endive* (often called escarole) – bunchy head of broad leaves that do not curl at tips; dark green outer leaves, pale yellow heart; not as bitter as curly endive. *French endive* (Witloof chicory) – thin, elongated stalk usually bleached white while growing.

Kale – Curly-leafed green of cabbage family; dark green; may have slightly browned edges caused by cold weather in growing season. Trim off tough stems and bruised or wilted leaves; wash; drain; dry.

Parsley – Discard coarse stems and bruised leaves; wash gently but thoroughly in cold water; drain and shake off excess water; pat dry. Store in tightly covered jar or plastic bag in refrigerator.

Spinach – Discard tough stems, roots and bruised or wilted leaves. Wash leaves thoroughly by lifting up and down several times in a large amount of cold water. Lift leaves out of water each time before pouring off water; repeat in clean water until all sand and grit are removed. Drain; pat dry.

Watercress – See PARSLEY. Watercress also may be stored before it is washed. Stand a tied bunch in a jar or bowl holding enough cold water to reach about halfway up stems. Cover and store in refrigerator. When using, snip off amount needed, rinse, drain and shake off excess water. Or store cleaned water cress in a plastic bag in refrigerator.

Other Greens – *Field salad* – spoon-shaped leaves; *finocchio* – anise-flavored stalk (like celery); *Swiss chard* – use tops only (like beet greens); – *beet, dandelion, mustard, turnip greens* – use tops only.

SALAD DRESSINGS – A twist of the wrist and a turn or two of the imagination – endless variations are possible from the basic French, mayonnaise and cooked dressings. Others are the sweet or sour cream, cream or cottage cheese and yogurt dressings and the bacon-vinegar type for wilted greens.

Mayonnaise has caused many a tear when it has broken or separated because the oil was added too rapidly at the beginning. The problem is to re-form (re-emulsify) the mayonnaise; the solution is to gradually add the mayonnaise, beating constantly, to 1 egg yolk, 1 tablespoon cold water, small quantity of vinegar or small portion of good mayonnaise. Mayonnaise will separate if frozen or kept in the coldest part of the refrigerator.

French dressings need to be shaken before using to mix thoroughly and re-form the emulsion.

Salad dressings should be stored covered in a cool place or in the refrigerator.

Vegetable Salads

Mixed Vegetable Salad

ABOUT
8 SERVINGS

1 cup diced cooked potatoes
1½ cups cooked sliced carrots
1½ cups cooked whole or cut green beans (fresh, frozen, or canned)
1½ cups cooked green peas (fresh, frozen, or canned)
1 cup sliced or diced cooked beets
Bottled Italian-style salad dressing
Lettuce
1 cup sliced celery
1 small onion, chopped
2 hard-cooked eggs, chopped
¾ cup small pimento-stuffed olives
¾ cup mayonnaise
¼ cup chili sauce
1 teaspoon lemon juice

1. Put potatoes, carrots, beans, peas, and beets into separate bowls. Pour salad dressing over each vegetable; chill thoroughly.
2. To serve, drain vegetables and arrange in a lettuce-lined salad bowl along with celery, onion, eggs, and olives.
3. Blend mayonnaise, chili sauce, and lemon juice. Pass with the salad.

Vegetable Salad with Yogurt Dressing

4 SERVINGS

¾ cup Low-Fat Yogurt (page 72)
2 tablespoons snipped parsley
½ cup finely chopped dill pickle
½ cup chopped tomato
1 teaspoon salt
1 cup sliced radishes
1 medium zucchini, shredded
2 medium carrots, shredded
1 large beet, shredded

1. Mix yogurt, parsley, pickle, chopped tomato, and salt; refrigerate covered 1 hour.
2. Arrange radish slices around edge of a serving plate. Arrange zucchini, carrots, and beet decoratively in center of plate. Serve yogurt mixture with salad.

Roquefort-Vegetable Salad

6 SERVINGS

Crisp salad greens
1 small onion, sliced
1 cup sliced raw cauliflower
1 can (16 ounces) cut green
beans, chilled and drained
1 can (13 to 15 ounces) green
asparagus spears, chilled
and drained
Roquefort-Mayonnaise Dressing, below

1. Half-fill six individual salad bowls with the greens. Arrange vegetables on greens.
2. Accompany with a bowl of the dressing garnished with snipped **parsley.**

Roquefort-Mayonnaise Dressing: Blend **3 ounces cream cheese,** softened, in a bowl with **3 ounces Roquefort cheese,** crumbled. Stir in ½ **cup light cream,** ½ **cup mayonnaise,** ½ **teaspoon Worcestershire sauce,** ¼ **teaspoon garlic powder,** and ¼ **teaspoon dry mustard.** Beat until fluffy and chill.
ABOUT 1½ CUPS DRESSING

Vegetable Platter Vinaigrette

8 TO 10 SERVINGS

1 pound fresh green beans
1 small head cauliflower
Chicken Stock (see page 76)
1 cup Vinaigrette Dressing
(see page 71)
1 pint cherry tomatoes,
halved
Salt
Freshly ground pepper
1 medium red onion, thinly
sliced

1. Steam green beans and whole cauliflower in separate covered saucepans in 1 inch of stock until tender (about 15 minutes). Drain. Mix beans with ½ cup dressing; refrigerate covered 3 hours, stirring occasionally.
2. Drain beans and tomatoes; reserve dressing. Place cauliflower in center of a platter; arrange beans and tomatoes around cauliflower. Sprinkle vegetables lightly with salt and pepper. Arrange onion slices over beans and tomatoes. Cut cauliflower into wedges to serve. Pass reserved dressing.

Caesar Salad

6 TO 8 SERVINGS

¼ cup olive oil
¼ cup lemon juice
¼ teaspoon Worcestershire
Sauce
Curly endive
Lettuce
Romaine
Watercress
2 slices toasted bread
2 tablespoons olive oil
3 cloves garlic, cut in halves
¾ cup grated Parmesan cheese
½ teaspoon dry mustard
½ teaspoon salt
¼ teaspoon pepper
1 egg
Anchovy fillets (about 12 to 15)

1. Chill a large salad bowl.
2. For Dressing – Mix together ¼ cup olive oil, lemon juice and 1 clove garlic.
3. Chill in refrigerator 1 hr.
4. For Salad Greens – Rinse curly endive, lettuce, romaine and watercress, discarding bruised leaves, drain and dry thoroughly.
5. Using as much of each green as desired, tear into pieces enough greens to yield about 2 qts. Put into a large plastic bag or a vegetable freshener. Chill in refrigerator at least 1 hr.
6. When the dressing is chilled, remove and reserve that garlic. Return dressing to refrigerator.
7. For Croutons – Stack and, if desired, trim crusts from bread.
8. Cut bread into ½-inch cubes.
9. Heat 2 tablespoons olive oil over low heat in a large skillet.
10. Add the clove of garlic from the dressing, with an additional clove of garlic, cut in halves.
11. Add bread cubes to the skillet and move and turn gently over medium heat until all sides of the cubes are lightly coated with oil and browned. Remove from heat.
12. To Complete Salad – Rub the salad bowl with cut surfaces of 1 clove garlic, cut in halves.

13. Turn chilled salad greens into the bowl. Sprinkle over greens a mixture of Parmesan cheese, dry mustard, salt and pepper.

14. Shake the chilled salad dressing well and pour it over the greens.

15. Break egg into a small bowl.

16. Add to the seasoned greens. Gentle turn and toss salad until greens are coated with dressing and no trace of egg remains. Add the croutons and toss lightly to mix thoroughly. Top with anchovy fillets (about 12 to 15).

17. Serve at once.

Blue Cheese Special: Follow recipe for Caesar Salad. Substitute ½ cup (about 2 oz.) crumbled **Blue cheese** for the Parmesan cheese. Omit dry mustard and anchovy fillets.

Red Vegetable Salad

4 TO 6
SERVINGS

1 pint cherry tomatoes,
  stems removed, cut in half
20 radishes, sliced
1 small red onion, sliced
3 tablespoons wine vinegar
2 teaspoons salad oil
1 teaspoon salt
2 teaspoons snipped fresh
  mint
⅛ teaspoon freshly ground
  white pepper
Lettuce leaves

1. Combine all ingredients except lettuce leaves in a medium bowl; refrigerate covered 2 hours, stirring occasionally.

2. Serve vegetables on lettuce.

Red Vegetable Salad

Garden Vegetables in Sweet Seasoned Vinegar

4 SERVINGS

1½ cups very thinly sliced baby cucumbers
2 cups very thinly sliced broccoli stalks
½ cup cider vinegar
½ teaspoon salt
¼ teaspoon freshly ground pepper
1½ teaspoons sugar
Salad greens

1. Arrange vegetable slices in a shallow glass dish. Shake remaining ingredients except salad greens in a covered jar; pour over vegetables. Refrigerate covered 30 minutes; stir occasionally. Drain; marinade can be strained and refrigerated for use again.
2. Serve vegetables on salad greens.

Green Salad

ABOUT 6 SERVINGS

1 large head lettuce, or an equal amount of another salad green (curly endive, romaine, escarole, chicory, or dandelion greens)
1 clove garlic
Italian Dressing (see page 71)

1. Wash lettuce in cold water, removing core, separating leaves, and removing any bruised leaves. Drain; dry thoroughly and carefully. Tear lettuce into bite-size pieces, put into a plastic bag, and chill 1 hour.
2. Just before serving, cut garlic in half and rub a wooden bowl. Put greens in bowl and pour on desired amount of dressing. Turn and toss the greens until well coated with dressing and no dressing remains in the bottom of the bowl.

Green Salad with Anchovy Dressing: Follow recipe for Green Salad. Add **2 tomatoes,** cut in wedges, **¼ cup diced celery,** and **½ cup chopped ripe olives** to lettuce in bowl. Toss with **Anchovy Dressing.**

Mixed Salad: Follow recipe for Green Salad. Add **¼ cup chopped cucumber, ¼ cup chopped celery, ¼ cup sliced radishes,** and **¼ cup chopped ripe olives** to lettuce before tossing with dressing.

Wilted Lettuce

ABOUT 8 SERVINGS

1 large head lettuce
6 slices bacon, diced
½ cup water
¼ cup cider vinegar
2 tablespoons heavy cream
1 tablespoon sugar
¼ teaspoon salt

1. Tear lettuce into pieces into a bowl; set aside.
2. Fry bacon until crisp in a skillet; reserve ¼ cup drippings. Drain bacon on absorbent paper; set aside.
3. Stir the remaining ingredients into drippings in skillet. Heat mixture just to boiling, stirring constantly.
4. Immediately pour vinegar mixture over the lettuce and toss lightly to coat thoroughly. Top with the bacon.

Green Goddess Salad

6 TO 8 SERVINGS

Green Goddess Salad Dressing (page 72)
Salad greens (such as lettuce, curly endive or escarole)

1. Prepare and chill green goddess salad dressing.
2. Rinse salad greens, discard bruised leaves, drain and dry.
3. Using as much of each green as desired, tear into pieces enough greens to yield about 2 quarts. Put into a large plastic bag or vegetable freshener. Chill in refrigerator.
4. When ready to serve, turn salad greens into a chilled bowl. Add the dressing and gently turn and toss until greens are evenly coated.
5. Serve immediately.

Green Goddess Salad with Crab Meat: Follow recipe for Green Goddess Salad. Drain, remove and discard bony tissue, and separate contents of 2 6½-ounce cans **crab meat** (about 2⅔ cups, drained). Lightly toss crab meat with salad greens.

Tossed Supper Salad

8 TO 10 SERVINGS

Dressing:
1 cup salad oil
½ cup cider vinegar
1 teaspoon salt
1 teaspoon sugar
½ teaspoon onion salt
¼ teaspoon crushed tarragon
¼ teaspoon paprika
¼ teaspoon dry mustard
¼ teaspoon celery salt
⅛ teaspoon garlic salt
⅛ teaspoon ground black pepper

Salad:
2 cans (6½ or 7 ounces each) tuna
½ head lettuce
1 cup spinach leaves, washed
1 cup diced celery
¾ cup chopped green pepper
½ cup cooked green peas
4 sweet pickles, chopped
4 radishes, thinly sliced
2 hard-cooked eggs, sliced
2 tablespoons chopped pimento
2 tomatoes, rinsed and cut in eighths
1 teaspoon salt
Tomato wedges
Ripe olives

1. For dressing, put oil and vinegar into a jar; mix salt, sugar, and seasonings; add to jar, cover, and shake well. Refrigerate until needed. Shake before using.
2. For salad, drain tuna well and separate into small chunks; put into a bowl. Toss tuna with ½ cup prepared dressing; cover and refrigerate 1 to 2 hours.
3. Tear lettuce and spinach into pieces and put into a large bowl. Add celery, green pepper, peas, pickles, radishes, eggs, and pimento; add the tuna with its dressing and tomatoes. Sprinkle with salt. Toss lightly until ingredients are mixed and lightly coated with dressing; add more dressing, if desired.
4. Garnish with tomato wedges and ripe olives.

Raw Broccoli Salad

4 SERVINGS

3 cups raw bite-size pieces broccoli spears
½ cup Low-Fat Yogurt (see page 72)
½ teaspoon freshly ground pepper
2 ounces Cheddar cheese, shredded
1 large carrot, cut in thin slices

Mix broccoli with yogurt, salt, and pepper. Spoon mixture on 4 salad plates. Sprinkle tops of salads with cheese; arrange carrot slices around salads.

Broccoli Salad

ABOUT
3 SERVINGS

1 pound broccoli
3 tablespoons olive oil
3 tablespoons lemon juice
1 medium clove garlic
¼ teaspoon salt
⅛ teaspoon pepper

1. Trim off leaves and bottoms of broccoli stalks, and split thick stems lengthwise. Cook, covered, in a small amount of salted water until just tender. Drain and chill.
2. Combine olive oil, lemon juice, garlic, salt, and pepper. Drizzle over thoroughly chilled broccoli and serve.

Cauliflower Salad: Follow recipe for Broccoli Salad. Substitute **1 medium head cauliflower** for broccoli. Peel and dice **1 boiled potato**; combine with cauliflower and chill. Substitute **wine vinegar** for the lemon juice and add ¼ **teaspoon oregano**

Green Bean Salad: Follow recipe for Broccoli Salad. Clean and cook ½ **pound green beans** and substitute for broccoli. Use wine vinegar instead of lemon juice.

Asparagus Salad: Follow recipe for Broccoli Salad. Clean and cook **1 pound asparagus** and substitute for the broccoli.

Beet Salad

4 OR 5
SERVINGS

1 16 ounce can sliced beets (about 2 cups, drained)
½ cup vinegar
¼ cup reserved beet liquid
2 tablespoons sugar
1½ teaspoons salt
1 teaspoon caraway seeds
⅛ teaspoon freshly ground pepper

1. Drain contents of can sliced beets, reserving liquid.
2. Place the beets into a 1-quart bowl and add a mixture of vinegar, beet liquid, sugar, salt, caraway seeds, and pepper.
3. Toss beets lightly in this salad marinade. Cover bowl and place into refrigerator to marinate 1 or 2 days; carefully turn beets occasionally.
4. Serve beets with some of the marinade.

Beet Salad with Horseradish: Follow recipe for Beet Salad. Add 1 or 2 tablespoons **freshly grated horseradish** or ¼ cup **prepared horseradish** to beets with the seasonings.

Beet Mousse

4 SERVINGS

8 medium beets
1 tablespoon vinegar
1½ teaspoons unflavored gelatin
¼ cup orange juice
½ cup instant nonfat dry-milk solids
2 to 3 ice cubes
1½ teaspoons prepared horseradish
Salad greens

1. Cut greens from beets; discard. Simmer beets in 2 inches water and vinegar until tender (about 30 minutes). Slip off skins. Cut thin slice from bottoms of beets; hollow out centers with melon-baller, leaving ½-inch shells; reserve centers. Refrigerate beets until chilled.
2. Sprinkle gelatin over orange juice in a small saucepan; let stand 5 minutes. Set over low heat, stirring occasionally, until gelatin is dissolved (about 3 minutes). Pour gelatin mixture into a food processor or blender; add beet centers and dry-milk solids. Process, adding ice cubes one at a time, until mixture is the consistency of thick whipped cream. Stir in horseradish. Fill beets with mixture; refrigerate until serving time. Serve on salad greens.

Green Bean and Onion Salad

6 SERVINGS

1 pound small boiling onions
1½ pounds fresh green beans
Chicken Stock (see page 76)
½ cup Mock Crème Fraîche
  (see page 78)
¼ cup low-fat cottage cheese
2 tablespoons snipped fresh
  chives
1 teaspoon snipped fresh or
  ½ teaspoon dried thyme
  leaves
1 teaspoon snipped fresh or
  ½ teaspoon dried mar-
  joram leaves
Salt
Freshly ground pepper
Juice of ½ lemon

1. Simmer onions and beans in 1 inch of stock in a covered saucepan until tender (15 to 18 minutes). Drain; refrigerate covered until chilled (about 2 hours).
2. Mix remaining ingredients except salt, pepper, and lemon juice; refrigerate covered until chilled.
3. Arrange vegetables on a platter; sprinkle lightly with salt and pepper. Squeeze lemon juice over. Spoon sauce over or pass sauce separately.

Antipasto Salad

6 TO 8
SERVINGS

1 quart assorted salad greens
1 package (10 ounces) frozen
  baby carrots in butter,
  cooked and drained
1 can (8¾ ounces) chickpeas or
  garbanzos, rinsed and
  drained
1 can (8¾ ounces) red kidney
  beans, rinsed and drained
1 jar (6 ounces) marinated
  artichoke hearts, drained
  and halved
½ cup sliced fresh mushrooms
½ cup drained pitted ripe
  olives
Seasoned Walnuts (below)
1 jar (4 ounces) pimiento, cut in
  strips
8 slices cooked ham or ham
  luncheon loaf, cut in strips
Dressing (below)

1. Arrange greens on serving platter.
2. Atop greens, arrange carrots, chickpeas, kidney beans, artichokes, mushrooms, and olives in separate mounds around the edge. Center with Seasoned Walnuts.
3. Make divisions between mounds with pimiento and ham strips. Serve with dressing.

Seasoned Walnuts: In a skillet, brown 1 cup walnut halves in 1 tablespoon salad oil. Sprinkle with a dash each of garlic salt and thyme.

Dressing: Measure into a jar ¾ cup salad oil, ⅓ cup red wine vinegar, 1 tablespoon Parmesan cheese, 1 teaspoon seasoned salt, ½ teaspoon each basil, seasoned pepper, and dry mustard, and ¼ teaspoon garlic powder. Shake well.
ABOUT 1¼ CUPS DRESSING

Pickled Pepper Salad

6 TO 8
SERVINGS

2 cups sliced pickled red
  peppers
¾ cup chopped celery
½ cup sliced ripe olives
8 anchovy fillets, chopped
2 tablespoons olive oil
2 tablespoons wine vinegar
¼ teaspoon oregano
⅛ teaspoon salt
¼ teaspoon pepper

1. Gently combine the red peppers, celery, olives, and anchovy fillets. Mix oil, vinegar, oregano, salt, and pepper; pour over the red pepper mixture. Toss gently.
2. Serve very cold.

Stuffed Eggplant Salad

6 SERVINGS

2 large eggplants
4 medium tomatoes, peeled and diced
⅓ cup thinly sliced green onion
⅓ cup olive or salad oil
½ cup fresh lemon juice
¼ cup chopped parsley
1 tablespoon sugar
2½ teaspoons salt
2 teaspoons oregano
¼ teaspoon ground black pepper

1. Wash and dry eggplants; place on a cookie sheet. Bake in a 375°F oven 35 to 45 minutes, or until tender when pierced with a fork. Cool.
2. Cut a thin lengthwise slice from the side of each eggplant; carefully spoon out pulp. Chill shells.
3. Dice pulp and put into a bowl. Add tomatoes, green onion, oil, lemon juice, parsley, sugar, salt, oregano, and pepper; toss to mix. Chill.
4. Before serving, drain off excess liquid from salad mixture. Spoon salad into shells.

Celery Whirls

ABOUT 1½ DOZEN WHIRLS

1 medium-size bunch celery
4 oz. Roquefort or Blue cheese (about 1 cup, crumbled)
3 oz. (1 pkg.) cream cheese, softened
1 tablespoon mayonnaise
2 teaspoons lemon juice
1 teaspoon onion juice
¼ teaspoon garlic salt
Few grains cayenne pepper
4 oz. Cheddar cheese (about 1 cup, grated)
3 oz. (1 pkg.) cream cheese, softened
3 tablespoons milk or cream
1½ teaspoons dry mustard
½ teaspoon salt
Few grains pepper
Few drops Tabasco

1. Clean celery.
2. Set aside to drain on absorbent paper while preparing one of the cheese stuffers.
3. **For Roquefort or Blue Cheese Stuffer** – Crumble Roquefort or blue cheese and set aside.
4. Thoroughly blend together 3 oz. cream cheese and mayonnaise.
5. Add crumbled cheese and beat until mixture is thoroughly blended. Blend in lemon juice and onion juice and a mixture of garlic salt and cayenne pepper.
6. Mix thoroughly.
7. **For Cheddar Cheese Stuffer** – Grate cheese and set aside.
8. Thoroughly blend together 3 oz. cream cheese and milk or cream.
9. Add grated cheese and beat until mixture is thoroughly blended. Blend in a mixture of dry mustard, salt and pepper.
10. Stir in a few drops of Tabasco.
11. Mix thoroughly.
12. **To Complete Whirls** – Fill full-length crisp stalks of

celery with one of the stuffers. Rearrange filled stalks in natural shape of celery bunch. Wrap bunch tightly in waxed paper, moisture-vapor-proof material or aluminum foil, and set in refrigerator to chill for several hours.

13. Cut into crosswise slices ¼ to ½ in. thick.

Zucchini Vinaigrette

ABOUT
6 SERVINGS

5 or 6 medium zucchini
1 package Italian salad dressing
   mix
¼ cup white wine vinegar
½ cup salad oil
2 tablespoons finely chopped
   green pepper
2 tablespoons finely chopped
   parsley
¼ cup finely chopped green
   onion
3 tablespoons sweet pickle
   relish

1. Cut ends from each zucchini and slice lengthwise into 6 pieces. Cook in a small amount of boiling salted water about 3 minutes, or until crisp-tender. Drain if necessary and cool; put into a shallow dish.

2. While zucchini is cooling, combine the remaining ingredients in a jar with a tight-fitting lid. Cover and shake vigorously to mix well.

3. Pour vinaigrette sauce over zucchini. Chill 4 hours or overnight. Serve with Grill-Baked Eggs au Gratin.

Asparagus Vinaigrette

6 SERVINGS

1 envelope herb-flavored oil-
   and-vinegar salad dressing
   mix
Tarragon-flavored white
   wine vinegar
Water
Salad oil
2 tablespoons chopped
   parsley
1 tablespoon finely chopped
   chives
2 teaspoons capers
1 hard-cooked egg, finely
   chopped
Cooked asparagus spears,
   chilled

1. Prepare salad dressing mix as directed on package, using vinegar, water, and salad oil.

2. Using 1 cup of the dressing, mix well with parsley, chives, capers and egg. Chill thoroughly.

3. To serve, arrange chilled asparagus in six bundles on a chilled serving plate lined with **Boston lettuce.** Garnish each bundle with a **pimento strip.** Complete platter with **cucumber slices** and **radish roses.** Mix dressing well before spooning over asparagus.

Guacamole I

ABOUT
2 CUPS
GUACAMOLE

2 very ripe avocados
1 medium fresh tomato
1 small onion, chopped
   (about ⅓ cup)
2 tablespoons lemon juice
1 teaspoon salt
1 to 2 teaspoons chili powder

1. Peel avocados and mash pulp, leaving a few small lumps throughout.

2. Peel and chop tomato and add to mashed avocado. Add onion, lemon juice, salt, and chili powder to taste. If not serving immediately, refrigerate in covered bowl, with avocado pits immersed in guacamole; this is said to help keep avocado from darkening on standing.

3. Serve on lettuce as a salad, as a "dip" with tostada chips, or as a condiment to top taco fillings.

Note: If you prefer a smoother guacamole, ingredients may be blended to desired consistency.

Guacamole II

ABOUT
3 CUPS DIP

2 large ripe avocados
3 tablespoons lemon juice
1 medium tomato
1 slice onion
1 small green chili
1 small clove garlic, minced
⅛ teaspoon coriander
Salt

1. Halve avocados, peel, remove pits, and cut avocado into pieces. Put into an electric blender with lemon juice.
2. Peel, halve, and seed tomato. Add to blender along with onion, chili, garlic, coriander, and salt to taste. Blend.
3. Serve as a dip with **corn chips, cauliflowerets,** and **carrot** and **celery sticks.**

Avocados Stuffed with Cauliflower Salad

6 SERVINGS

2 cups very small, crisp raw
   cauliflowerets
1 cup cooked green beans
½ cup sliced ripe olives
¼ cup chopped pimento
¼ cup chopped onion
Oil and Vinegar Dressing
Salt to taste
6 small lettuce leaves
3 large ripe avocados
Lemon wedges

1. Combine all ingredients, except lettuce, avocados, and lemon wedges; stir gently until evenly mixed and coated with dressing.
2. Refrigerate at least 1 hour before serving.
3. When ready to serve, peel, halve, and remove pits from avocados. Place a lettuce leaf on each serving plate; top with avocado half filled with a mound of cauliflower salad. Serve with lemon wedges.

Pimento Cheese-Avocado Salad

8 SERVINGS

Salad:
4 ripe avocados
Lemon juice
1 jar (7 ounces) whole
   pimentos, drained
⅓ cup fresh parsley, cleaned
   and trimmed (3 tablespoons
   chopped)
1 package (8 ounces) cream
   cheese, cut in quarters
1 tablespoon capers
Pinch cayenne pepper
½ teaspoon salt
⅛ teaspoon pepper
Salad greens

Dressing:
1 whole pimento, drained
½ cup mayonnaise
½ cup sour cream
¼ teaspoon salt
⅛ teaspoon pepper
2 tablespoons lemon juice

1. For salad, cut avocados into halves, peel, and remove pits. Enlarge the pit cavities with a spoon, reserving scooped-out avocado. Score the surfaces of cavities with a fork. Brush surface (except cavities) with lemon juice.
2. Pat pimentos dry with a paper towel. Keep pimentos in one piece. Line the avocado cavities with the pimentos and trim evenly around the edges. Set leftover pimento aside.
3. Using **steel blade** of food processor, process parsley until chopped. Set aside.
4. Using **plastic blade** of food processor, process cream cheese until smooth. Add 2 tablespoons chopped parsley, scooped-out avocado, leftover pimento, capers, cayenne pepper, salt, and pepper. Process until thoroughly blended.
5. Fill the lined avocado with the cheese mixture, spreading it smoothly on the top. Cover and chill thoroughly.
6. For dressing, using **plastic blade,** add all ingredients to the bowl and process until thoroughly blended. Chill thoroughly.
7. When ready to serve, halve each filled avocado shell lengthwise and arrange quarters on crisp salad greens. Serve with dressing on the side.

Avocados Stuffed With Cauliflower Salad

Cucumber Salad

6 TO 8
SERVINGS

2 medium-size (about 1¼ pounds) cucumbers, washed and pared
2 teaspoons salt
3 tablespoons vinegar
3 tablespoons water
½ teaspoon sugar
¼ teaspoon paprika
¼ teaspoon pepper
½ clove garlic, minced
¼ teaspoon paprika

1. Slice cucumbers thinly into a bowl.
2. Sprinkle salt over the cucumber slices.
3. Mix lightly and set cucumbers aside for 1 hour.
4. Meanwhile, mix vinegar, water, sugar, ¼ teaspoon paprika, pepper and garlic together and set aside.
5. Squeeze cucumber slices, a few at a time (discarding liquid), and put into a bowl. Pour the vinegar mixture over the cucumbers and toss lightly. Sprinkle ¼ teaspoon paprika onto cucumbers.
6. Chill the salad in refrigerator for 1 to 2 hours.

Cucumber Salad with Sour Cream: Follow recipe for Cucumber Salad. Blend in 1 cup **thick sour cream** after the vinegar mixture.

Cucumber Salad with Onions: Follow recipe for Cucumber Salad or variation. Omit garlic. Cut off root ends from 3 or 4 fresh **green onions or scallions.** Trim green tops down to 2- or 3-inches, removing any wilted or bruised parts; peel and rinse. Slice onions by holding on hard surface and cutting across all with sharp knife. Add sliced onions to cucumber slices before adding the vinegar mixture.

Oriental Cucumber Salad

4 SERVINGS

10 baby cucumbers (about 3 inches long), sliced in very thin rounds
1 bunch green onions, tops only, finely chopped
2 teaspoons honey or sugar
2 teaspoons toasted sesame seed
½ cup distilled white vinegar
½ teaspoon sesame oil
5 tablespoons light soy sauce
Salad greens

1. Arrange cucumber and onion in a shallow glass dish. Shake remaining ingredients except salad greens in a covered jar; pour over the vegetables. Refrigerate for 2 hours, stirring occasionally.
2. Drain cucumber and onion; marinade can be strained and refrigerated for use again. Serve salad on lettuce or other salad greens.

Piquant Cucumber Slices

ABOUT
4 SERVINGS

2 tablespoons sugar
1 teaspoon salt
⅛ teaspoon white pepper
1 teaspoon celery seed
¼ cup cider vinegar
1 tablespoon lemon juice
1 cucumber, rinsed (do not pare)
¼ cup coarsely chopped onion
2 tablespoons chopped parsley

1. Combine the sugar, salt, white pepper, celery seed, vinegar, and lemon juice in a bowl; blend thoroughly.
2. Score cucumber by drawing tines of a fork lengthwise over entire surface. Cut into ⅛-inch slices.
3. Add cucumber to vinegar mixture with onion and parsley; toss to coat evenly.
4. Chill thoroughly, turning several times.

Cucumber and Tomato Salad

6 TO 8
SERVINGS

3 firm-ripe homegrown
  tomatoes, cut in wedges
3 pickle cucumbers (as
  straight as possible), pared
  and sliced ¼ inch thick
4 scallions, finely chopped
¼ pound feta cheese,
  crumbled
Kalamata olives (about 8)
Oregano and freshly dried
  dill, a generous pinch of
  each
Salt and pepper to taste
3 tablespoons wine vinegar
⅓ cup olive oil

1. In a salad bowl, combine tomatoes, cucumbers, scallions, cheese, and olives. Season with oregano, dill, salt, and pepper.
2. Combine vinegar and olive oil in a small jar; shake well. Add to salad and toss.

Tomato-Cream Slaw

ABOUT
6 SERVINGS

1 cup sour cream
¼ cup mayonnaise
½ cup tomato sauce
2 tablespoons cider vinegar
2 tablespoons sugar
1 teaspoon celery seed
1 small head cabbage,
  coarsely shredded

1. Combine in a bowl, the sour cream, mayonnaise, tomato sauce, vinegar, sugar, and celery seed. Refrigerate at least 1 hour for flavors to blend and dressing to chill.
2. Put shredded cabbage into a bowl and chill.
3. Just before serving, pour the dressing over the cabbage and toss lightly to mix.

Sweet-Sour Beans in Tomato Shells

6 SERVINGS

⅓ cup cider vinegar
2½ tablespoons dark brown
  sugar
½ teaspoon salt
1 can (16 ounces) diagonally
  sliced green beans, drained
1 tablespoon finely chopped
  onion
6 tomato shells, chilled
1 tablespoon basil, crushed

1. Pour a mixture of the vinegar, brown sugar, and salt over the beans and onion in a bowl; toss lightly. Set in refrigerator to marinate 1 hour, tossing occasionally.
2. Sprinkle the inside of each tomato shell with crushed basil and **salt.** Spoon beans equally into tomato shells. Garnish with crisp **bacon curls.**

Salade à la Crème

ABOUT
6 SERVINGS

1 quart mixed greens (such
  as iceberg, Boston, or Bibb
  lettuce, romaine, escarole,
  or chicory)
½ cup sour cream
2 tablespoons chopped
  parsley
2 tablespoons dry white wine
  (such as chenin blanc)
½ teaspoon salt
⅛ teaspoon freshly ground
  pepper

1. Using only perfect leaves, wash, dry, tear into pieces, and chill greens before combining with dressing. Cold, dry leaves ensure a crisp salad.
2. Combine sour cream, parsley, wine, salt, and pepper.
3. At serving time, transfer greens to a large bowl, add dressing, and toss well.

Bacon-Bean Salad

ABOUT
12 SERVINGS

⅔ cup cider vinegar
¾ cup sugar
1 teaspoon salt
1 can (16 ounces) cut green beans
1 can (16 ounces) cut wax beans
1 can (16 ounces) kidney beans, thoroughly rinsed and drained
1 can (16 ounces) lima beans
1 medium-sized onion, quartered and finely sliced
1 medium-sized green pepper, chopped
½ teaspoon freshly ground black pepper
⅓ cup salad oil
1 pound bacon, cut in 1-inch squares (optional)

1. Blend vinegar, sugar, and salt in a small saucepan. Heat until the sugar is dissolved. Remove from heat and set aside.
2. Drain all beans and toss with onion, green pepper, vinegar mixture, and the pepper. Pour oil over all and toss to coat evenly. Store in a large covered container in refrigerator.
3. When ready to serve, fry bacon until crisp; drain on absorbent paper. Toss the bacon with bean mixture.

Hearty Bean Salad

4 TO 6
SERVINGS

1 can (15 ounces) kidney beans, drained
2 hard-cooked eggs, diced
¼ cup chopped onion
½ cup diced celery
⅓ cup drained sweet pickle relish
½ cup shredded sharp Cheddar cheese
½ cup sour cream
Lettuce

1. Mix kidney beans, eggs, onion, celery, relish, and cheese in a large bowl. Add sour cream and toss together lightly; chill.
2. Serve the salad on lettuce.

Kidney Bean-Mushroom Salad

8 TO 10
SERVINGS

2 cans (about 15 ounces each) kidney beans, drained and rinsed
2 cans or jars (4 or 4½ ounces each) sliced mushrooms, drained
1 to 1½ cups thinly sliced celery (cut diagonally)
½ cup golden raisins
¼ cup red wine vinegar
1 clove garlic, minced
4 drops Tabasco
½ teaspoon ground cardamom
½ teaspoon curry powder
½ teaspoon tarragon leaves, crushed
¼ cup olive oil or other salad oil

1. Combine kidney beans, mushrooms, celery, and raisins in a large bowl; toss lightly.
2. Pour vinegar into a bottle and add remaining ingredients. Cover and shake vigorously. Pour over vegetables and toss lightly until well mixed. Chill until ready to pack for the picnic.
3. If desired, sprinkle flaked or shredded coconut over salad before serving.

Red Kidney Bean Salad

ABOUT
4 SERVINGS

1 can (16 ounces) kidney beans
¼ cup wine vinegar
3 tablespoons olive oil
¼ teaspoon oregano
¼ teaspoon salt
⅛ teaspoon pepper
¼ cup sliced celery
2 tablespoons chopped onion
Lettuce cups

1. Thoroughly rinse and drain kidney beans.
2. Combine vinegar, oil, oregano, salt, and pepper; mix with beans. Blend in celery and onion; chill.
3. Serve in crisp lettuce cups.

Garbanzo Salad

ABOUT
6 SERVINGS

1 can (15 ounces) garbanzos, drained
¼ cup chopped parsley
1 can or jar (4 ounces) pimentos, drained and chopped
3 green onions, chopped
¼ cup wine vinegar
2 tablespoons olive or salad oil
1 teaspoon salt
½ teaspoon sugar
¼ teaspoon pepper

Combine all ingredients in a bowl; cover and refrigerate until chilled.

Garbanzo Bean Salad

10 TO 12
SERVINGS

2 cans (15 ounces each) garbanzos, drained (about 4 cups)
1 cup cut celery
2 green peppers, diced or slivered
2 or 3 tomatoes, peeled and cut in small pieces
½ cup finely chopped sweet onion
1 cup radish slices
¼ cup snipped parsley
1 cup quartered pitted ripe olives
1 envelope Italian salad dressing mix
2 teaspoons Worcestershire sauce
1 teaspoon ground coriander
¾ teaspoon lemon pepper marinade

1. Combine the vegetables and olives in a bowl; toss lightly and refrigerate to chill.
2. Meanwhile, prepare salad dressing following package directions, using wine vinegar and adding Worcestershire sauce and remaining ingredients with the mix. Shake thoroughly before using.
3. About 1 hour before serving, toss salad ingredients lightly with dressing until well mixed, then chill.

Potato Salad

6 SERVINGS

½ cup olive oil
3 tablespoons wine vinegar
1 teaspoon oregano, crushed
2 tablespoons chopped
 parsley
1 medium onion, finely sliced
5 large red potatoes
Salt and pepper to taste

1. Combine olive oil, vinegar, oregano, parsley, and onion. Mix well. Set aside to marinate.
2. Scrub potatoes. Boil them in salted water in their jackets. When just tender (about 40 minutes), remove and plunge into cold water so they can be handled at once. Peel while hot and cut into even slices.
3. Pour the dressing over the potatoes; toss lightly. Add salt and pepper.

Italian Potato Salad I

ABOUT
10 SERVINGS

1 package (2 pounds) frozen
 southern-style hash brown
 potatoes
1 package (9 ounces) frozen
 Italian green beans
1 teaspoon seasoned salt
¼ teaspoon pepper
⅔ cup bottled creamy Italian
 dressing
½ cup chopped celery
½ cup pitted ripe olives, cut
 in half crosswise
2 hard-cooked eggs, diced
2 tablespoons chopped green
 onion
½ teaspoon salt
1 cup cherry tomatoes, cut
 in half
1 cup shredded Provolone
 cheese (about 4 ounces)
Romaine leaves

1. Thaw hash brown potatoes.
2. Cook Italian green beans, following package directions, until just tender; drain.
3. Combine potatoes and beans in a bowl. Sprinkle with seasoned salt and pepper. Chill.
4. Combine dressing, celery, olives, eggs, onion, and salt in a large bowl. Add chilled vegetables and toss to coat with dressing. Lightly mix in tomatoes and cheese. Chill thoroughly to blend flavors, at least several hours.
5. To serve, spoon salad into a bowl lined with romaine.

Italian Potato Salad II

ABOUT
4 SERVINGS

2 medium potatoes, boiled,
 peeled, and diced
⅓ cup chopped celery
½ cup diced pared cucumber
½ cup chopped ripe olives
2 tablespoons minced onion
¾ cup Italian Dressing
 (page 71)
¼ teaspoon oregano

1. Lightly toss together the potatoes, celery, cucumber, olives, and onion. With a fork, thoroughly but carefully blend in the dressing mixed with oregano.
2. Cover the salad. Chill about 1 hour before serving.

Blue Ribbon Potato-Onion Salad

10 TO 12
SERVINGS

2 pounds potatoes (about 6
  medium), cooked and peeled
2½ tablespoons cider vinegar
1 tablespoon salad oil
1½ teaspoons salt
3 hard-cooked eggs, chopped
1 cup diced celery
1¾ cups dairy sour cream
½ teaspoon sugar
Few grains pepper
2 tablespoons cider vinegar
1½ teaspoons prepared
  mustard
½ cup grated onion (or blender
  puréed)
½ cup sliced ripe olives

1. Cut potatoes into ½-inch cubes and put into a bowl. Toss with a mixture of vinegar, oil, and salt. Add eggs, celery, and dressing; toss until mixed. Cover and chill thoroughly.
2. Combine remaining ingredients. Chill until ready to use.
3. Turn salad into a chilled salad bowl.

German Potato Salad

ABOUT
6 SERVINGS

12 slices bacon, diced and
  fried until crisp (reserve 6
  tablespoons drippings)
3 medium-sized onions,
  chopped (2 cups)
1 cup less 2 tablespoons
  cider vinegar
1½ tablespoons sugar
1½ teaspoons salt
¼ teaspoon pepper
2 to 3 lbs. potatoes, cooked,
  peeled, and cut in ¼-inch
  slices

1. Heat bacon drippings in a skillet. Add onion and cook until tender, stirring occasionally. Stir in vinegar, sugar, salt, monosodium glutamate, and pepper; heat to boiling. Mix in bacon.
2. Pour over potato slices in a serving dish and toss lightly to coat evenly. Garnish with snipped **parsley** and **paprika**. Serve hot.

German Potato Salad

Anchovy Potato Salad

4 TO 6
SERVINGS

Dressing
1 cup olive oil
½ cup wine vinegar
¼ teaspoon sugar
1 teaspoon dill
1 teaspoon marjoram
Pepper to taste

Salad
8 Anchovy Fillets or 1 can (2 ounces) anchovies preserved in olive oil, drained
1 bunch escarole, torn in bite-size pieces
2 potatoes, boiled and diced
1 small jar pickled beets, drained and diced
2 green peppers, cleaned and thinly sliced
4 scallions, minced
3 hard-cooked eggs, sliced, for garnish
1 teaspoon capers for garnish
Salt and pepper to taste

1. For dressing, combine all ingredients in a jar. Shake well. Refrigerate 1 or 2 hours before serving.
2. For salad, combine anchovies with remaining ingredients, except eggs, capers, salt, and pepper. Add the salad dressing and toss to coat. Garnish with eggs and capers. Season with salt and pepper.

Potato Salad with Wine

6 SERVINGS

2 pounds potatoes
2 teaspoons salt
Boiling water
1 cup white wine
1 stalk celery
⅓ cup olive oil
¼ cup chopped fresh dill
¼ cup chopped parsley
3 tablespoons lemon juice
2 tablespoons chopped chives
¼ teaspoon pepper

1. Cook potatoes with salt in enough boiling water to cover until tender, about 30 minutes. Peel and slice; put into a bowl.
2. Pour wine over potatoes; let stand 30 minutes.
3. Cook celery in a small amount of boiling water until soft. Press celery through a sieve. Combine 2 tablespoons cooking liquid and puréed celery, oil, dill, parsley, lemon juice, chives, and pepper.
4. Add celery mixture to potatoes; mix.

Hot Potato Salad

6 SERVINGS

6 medium boiling potatoes (2 pounds)
10 slices bacon (½ pound)
½ cup chopped onion
½ cup beer
1 to 1½ tablespoons sugar
1 to 1½ teaspoons salt
1 teaspoon celery seed

1. Place unpeeled potatoes in a large saucepan; add water to cover. Heat to boiling. Boil, uncovered, for 20 minutes, or until tender. Peel and cube; turn into a serving dish.
2. Meanwhile, cook bacon until crisp; leave drippings in skillet. Crumble bacon over potatoes.
3. Add onion to skillet. Sauté until tender. Add beer, sugar, salt, and celery seed. Heat to boiling, stirring occasionally. Pour over potatoes; toss lightly.

Fruited Carrot Salad

4 SERVINGS

4 carrots
1 cup unsweetened pineapple juice
2½ cups orange juice
Lettuce cups
Snipped mint

1. Pare carrots into strips with a vegetable peeler. Place in a shallow glass dish; pour fruit juices over. Refrigerate covered 6 hours or overnight, stirring occasionally.
2. Drain carrots, spoon into lettuce cups, and garnish with mint.

Fresh Bean Sprout Salad

4 TO 6 SERVINGS

1 pound fresh bean sprouts, rinsed (see Note)
2 medium carrots, shredded
1 tablespoon toasted sesame seed
2 teaspoons vegetable oil
⅓ cup distilled white vinegar
2 teaspoons sugar

1. Mix bean sprouts and carrots in a shallow glass dish.
2. Shake remaining ingredients in a covered jar; pour over vegetables.
3. Refrigerate covered 1½ hours; stir occasionally. Serve in shallow bowls.

Note: If fresh bean sprouts are not available, you can substitute **1 large pared, seeded, shredded cucumber.**

Shades o' Green Salad

6 SERVINGS

French Dressing (page 74)
3 ounces (about 3 cups) spinach
4 stalks Pascal celery
½ green pepper
1 cucumber, rinsed
½ head lettuce
2 tablespoons chopped chives
6 green olives
1 small avocado

1. Chill 6 individual salad bowls in refrigerator.
2. Prepare and chill French dressing.
3. Remove and discard tough stems, roots and bruised leaves from spinach.
4. Wash, drain and pat dry. Use part of the spinach to line the salad bowls. Set remainder aside.
5. Cut celery, pepper and cucumber into pieces or slices.
6. Rinse lettuce, drain and pat dry.
7. Tear lettuce and reserved spinach into pieces. Toss vegetables with lettuce, spinach and chives.
8. Add about ⅓ cup of the French dressing; toss lightly to coat greens evenly. (Store remaining dressing in a covered container in refrigerator.)
9. Arrange individual portions of salad in bowls.
10. Pit and slice olives.
11. Rinse, peel, cut into halves lengthwise, remove pit and slice avocado.
12. Garnish salads with avocado and olive slices.

Shades o' Green Salad

Salade Niçoise

6 TO 8
SERVINGS

Salad Dressing, below
3 medium-sized cooked
    potatoes, sliced
1 package (9 ounce) frozen
    green beans, cooked
1 clove garlic, cut in half
1 small head Boston lettuce
2 cans (6½ or 7 ounces each)
    tuna, drained
1 mild onion, quartered and
    thinly sliced
2 ripe tomatoes, cut in
    wedges
2 hard-cooked eggs,
    quartered
1 can (2 ounces) rolled an-
    chovy fillets, drained
¾ cup pitted ripe olives
1 tablespoon capers

1. Pour enough salad dressing over warm potato slices and cooked beans (in separate bowls) to coat vegetables.
2. Before serving, rub the inside of a large shallow salad bowl with the cut surface of the garlic. Line the bowl or a large serving platter with the lettuce.
3. Unmold the tuna in center of bowl and separate into chunks.
4. Arrange separate mounds of the potatoes, green beans, onion, tomatoes, and hard-cooked eggs in colorful grouping around the tuna. Garnish with anchovies, olives, and capers.
5. Pour dressing over all before serving.

Salad Dressing: Combine in a jar or bottle ½ cup olive oil or salad oil, 2 tablespoons red wine vinegar, a mixture of 1 teaspoon salt, ½ teaspoon pepper, and 1 teaspoon dry mustard, 1 tablespoon finely chopped chives, and 1 tablespoon finely chopped parsley. Shake vigorously to blend well before pouring over salad.
ABOUT ⅔ CUP

Russian Salad

6 SERVINGS

⅓ cup olive oil
3 tablespoons vinegar
1 cup diced cooked carrots
1 cup diced cooked beets
2 potatoes, cooked and diced
1 cup french-cut green
    beans, cooked and diced
1 cup cooked peas
¼ cup minced parsley
Mayonnaise
Salt and pepper to taste
2 teaspoons capers

1. Mix olive oil and vinegar and pour over vegetables; allow to marinate 1 to 2 hours. Drain. Discard dressing.
2. Mix vegetables and parsley with enough mayonnaise to bind together (about 1 cup). Season with salt and pepper. Garnish with capers to serve.

Warsaw Salad

8 TO 12
SERVINGS

1 cup mayonnaise
⅓ cup sour cream
1 tablespoon prepared
    mustard
2 cups julienne beets, cooked
    or canned
1½ cups kidney beans,
    cooked or canned
1½ cups cooked or canned
    peas
1 cup diced dill pickles
6 ounces (about 1¼ cups)
    cooked crab meat
3 scallions, chopped
1 hard-cooked egg, sliced
Carrot curls and radish
    roses to garnish

1. Combine mayonnaise, sour cream, and mustard in a large bowl.
2. Add remaining ingredients, except egg, carrots, and radishes; toss gently to mix.
3. Garnish with egg slices, carrot curls, and radish roses.

Salade Niçoise

Greek Salad in Peppers

4 SERVINGS

1 large tomato, chopped
1 green onion, sliced
⅛ teaspoon salt
1 teaspoon snipped fresh or
  ½ teaspoon dried basil
  leaves
1 tablespoon fresh lemon
  juice
4 small green peppers, cored
½ cup crumbled feta cheese
8 anchovies, drained and
  rinsed
8 lemon wedges

1. Mix tomato, onion, salt, basil, and lemon juice; refrigerate covered 1 hour.
2. Spoon half the tomato mixture into green peppers; layer cheese over tomatoes. Spoon remaining tomato mixture over cheese. Arrange 2 anchovies over top of each pepper. Serve with lemon wedges.

Greek Salad

8 SERVINGS

Salad Dressing:
⅓ cup olive oil
¼ cup wine vinegar
½ teaspoon salt
1 teaspoon oregano

Salad:
1 large head romaine,
  trimmed and torn in pieces
1 cucumber, pared and cut
  in 3½-inch pieces
1 small bunch radishes,
  cleaned and trimmed
2 small green peppers,
  trimmed and cored
1 can (8 ounces) whole beets,
  drained
4 tomatoes
⅓ pound feta cheese
Greek olives
Anchovy fillets (optional)

1. For salad dressing, mix all ingredients and refrigerate.
2. For salad, put romaine pieces in a large salad bowl.
3. Using **slicing disc** of food processor, slice cucumber, radishes, green pepper, and beets.
4. Cut tomatoes into quarters.
5. Using **plastic blade** of food processor, process feta cheese, using quick on/off motions, until crumbled.
6. Combine prepared salad ingredients with romaine in a bowl, sprinkle with crumbled feta cheese, and top with olives and, if desired, anchovy fillets. Pour salad dressing over salad and serve.

Greek Salad

Rose Salad

8 TO 12
SERVINGS

10 small potatoes (about 2½
  pounds), cooked
¼ cup olive oil
3 tablespoons lemon juice or
  vinegar
1 tablespoon water
1 tablespoon sugar
1 teaspoon salt
¼ teaspoon pepper
2 cups shell beans, cooked
  or canned
¼ pound sauerkraut,
  drained
4 stalks celery, sliced
  lengthwise
6 cups shredded red cabbage
Boiling water
3 tablespoons tarragon
  vinegar
4 cooked or canned beets,
  sliced

1. Slice potatoes. Mix olive oil, lemon juice, 1 tablespoon water, sugar, salt, and pepper. Pour over potatoes. Add beans, sauerkraut, and celery.
2. Add red cabbage to boiling water. Let stand 2 minutes. Drain well. Stir in tarragon vinegar; mix until cabbage is pink.
3. Mound red cabbage in center of a large platter. Arrange beet slices in cabbage to form a rose.
4. Place potatoes and other vegetables around edges. Use **celery** for rose stem. Garnish with **lettuce leaves.**

Red Cabbage-Apple Salad

4 SERVINGS

3 cups shredded red cabbage
1 red apple, cut in 1½ x
  ¼-inch strips
1 sweet red pepper, cut in
  1½ x ¼-inch strips
2 tablespoons cider vinegar
¼ cup apple juice
¼ teaspoon caraway seed
⅛ teaspoon salt
⅛ teaspoon freshly ground
  pepper
Salad greens

Mix all ingredients except salad greens in a medium bowl. Refrigerate covered 2 hours. Serve on salad greens or individual plates.

Sauerkraut Salad with Carrots and Apples

ABOUT
6 SERVINGS

¼ cup salad or olive oil
1½ teaspoons sugar
1 teaspoon caraway seed
½ teaspoon salt
1 teaspoon vinegar
1 pound sauerkraut, drained
2 medium tart apples,
  peeled, cored, and diced
¾ cup grated carrot

1. Combine oil, sugar, caraway seed, salt, and vinegar.
2. Rinse and drain sauerkraut well; chop. Stir into oil mixture.
3. Add apples and carrot; toss to mix.

Piquant Pepper-Cabbage Slaw

ABOUT
8 SERVINGS

¼ to ⅓ cup sugar
2 tablespoons flour
1 teaspoon salt
2 teaspoons dry mustard
2 eggs, fork beaten
1 cup milk, scalded
¾ cup cider vinegar
2 tablespoons butter or
  margarine
1 teaspoon celery seed
1 head chilled cabbage,
  finely shredded
1 green pepper, chopped
1 red pepper, chopped

1. Mix sugar, flour, salt, and dry mustard together in top of a double boiler. Blend in the eggs and milk. Cook over boiling water about 5 minutes, stirring frequently.
2. Stir in the vinegar, a small amount at a time. Cook and stir until mixture begins to thicken, then mix in butter and celery seed. Remove from heat; cool and chill thoroughly.
3. To serve, toss the cabbage and peppers with enough dressing to coat evenly (store remaining dressing); mound onto fresh **spinach leaves.**

Crunchy Peanut Cole Slaw

8 SERVINGS

3 cups finely chopped green
  cabbage
1 cup finely chopped red
  cabbage
1 cup finely chopped celery
1 cup coarsely chopped
  cauliflower
1 cup sour cream
1 cup mayonnaise
1 tablespoon sugar
1 teaspoon salt
1 tablespoon tarragon
  vinegar
½ cup finely chopped
  cucumber
¼ cup finely chopped green
  onion
¼ cup finely chopped green
  pepper
1 tablespoon butter or
  margarine
½ cup coarsely chopped
  salted peanuts
2 tablespoons shredded
  Parmesan cheese

1. Toss the green and red cabbage, celery, and cauliflower together and chill.
2. Combine the sour cream, mayonnaise, sugar, salt, vinegar, cucumber, green onion, and green pepper for the salad dressing and chill thoroughly.
3. Melt butter in a small skillet; add peanuts and heat several minutes until lightly browned. Remove from heat and immediately stir in the Parmesan cheese. Set aside.
4. Just before serving, toss chilled vegetables with the dressing and top with the peanut mixture.

Turnip-Carrot-Cabbage Slaw

ABOUT
6 SERVINGS

1 cup shredded white turnip
1 cup shredded carrot
2 cups finely shredded
  cabbage
¼ cup finely chopped onion
¼ cup chopped parsley
¼ teaspoon salt
⅛ teaspoon pepper
3 tablespoons mayonnaise

1. Toss vegetables together gently with a mixture of salt, pepper, and mayonnaise until vegetables are evenly coated.
2. Chill, covered, in refrigerator until ready to serve.

Sardine-Egg Salad-Stuffed Tomatoes

6 SERVINGS

6 tomatoes
2 cans (3¾ ounces each)
  Norwegian sardines
6 hard-cooked eggs, diced
2 tablespoons capers
¼ cup sour cream
2 tablespoons mayonnaise
1 tablespoon caper liquid
½ teaspoon dry mustard
¼ teaspoon salt

1. Rinse tomatoes (peel if desired) and chill thoroughly in refrigerator.
2. Drain 1 can of sardines, remove tails, and cut the sardines into pieces; reserve the other can of sardines for completing the salad. Lightly toss the sardines for completing the salad. Lightly toss the sardines with the eggs and capers.
3. Combine the sour cream, mayonnaise, caper liquid, dry mustard, and salt. Add to egg-sardine mixture and toss lightly to mix well. Chill thoroughly.
4. When both the mixture and tomatoes are thoroughly chilled, cut a slice from the top of each tomato. Using a spoon, remove seeds. Invert shells to drain. Sprinkle insides with **seasoned salt** before stuffing. Fill center of tomatoes with the egg-sardine mixture.
5. Choose greenest **lettuce leaves** and use to line salad plates. Set tomatoes on lettuce. Place one sardine across each stuffed tomato and garnish with sprigs of **watercress.**

Orange-Pea Salad

6 SERVINGS

2 packages (10 ounces each)
  frozen green peas
1⅓ cups chopped celery
½ teaspoon dried leaf
  tarragon
¼ cup sour cream
2 teaspoons grated orange
  peel
2 tablespoons thawed frozen
  orange juice concentrate
1 teaspoon salt
½ teaspoon sugar
Salad greens
Orange sections

1. Cook peas according to package directions. Drain and cool. Mix with celery, tarragon, sour cream, orange peel, orange concentrate, salt, and sugar. Chill.
2. Line a serving bowl with salad greens, spoon in pea salad, and garnish with orange sections.

Meat, Seafood, and Poultry Salads

Greek-Style Lamb-and-Olive Salad

6 SERVINGS

Greek-Style Salad Dressing:
½ cup olive or salad oil
1 cup red wine vinegar
3 to 4 tablespoons honey
1½ teaspoons salt
⅛ teaspoon dry mustard
2 teaspoons crushed dried
    mint leaves
¼ teaspoon crushed oregano
¼ teaspoon crushed thyme
¼ teaspoon anise seed

Salad:
1½ pounds roast lamb,
    trimmed of fat and cut in
    strips
Curly endive
1 large cucumber, pared and
    sliced
4 medium tomatoes, sliced
    and quartered
1 cup pitted ripe olives

1. For dressing, mix oil, vinegar, honey, salt, dry mustard, mint, oregano, thyme, and anise.
2. Pour the dressing over cooked lamb in a bowl, cover, and marinate in refrigerator at least 1 hour, or until thoroughly chilled.
3. To serve, arrange curly endive in a large salad bowl. Toss cucumber, tomatoes, and olives with some of the dressing and turn into salad bowl. Spoon meat over vegetables and pour more dressing over all.

Beef Salad Acapulco

4 TO 6
SERVINGS

3 cups cooked beef strips
¾ cup salad oil
½ cup red wine vinegar
1½ teaspoons salt
¼ teaspoon ground pepper
⅛ teaspoon cayenne pepper
1 tablespoon chili powder
Salad greens
Avocado slices, brushed with
    marinade
Onion and green pepper
    rings
Tomato wedges
Ripe olives

1. Put beef strips into a shallow dish. Combine oil, vinegar, salt, pepper, cayenne pepper, and chili powder in a bottle; cover and shake vigorously. Pour over beef strips. Cover; marinate several hours or overnight.
2. Remove beef from marinade and arrange on crisp greens on chilled salad plates. Garnish with avocado slices, onion rings, green pepper rings, tomato wedges, and ripe olives. Serve the marinade as the dressing.

Roast Beef Salad

ABOUT
4 SERVINGS

1 egg
3 cups cold roast beef cubes
¼ cup quick meat broth
  (below)
1 uncooked egg yolk
1 tablespoon cider vinegar
1 teaspoon dry mustard
⅓ cup salad oil
2 tablespoons chopped parsley
1 tablespoon finely chopped
  anchovy fillets
1 teaspoon capers
¾ teaspoon thyme

1. Hard-cook 1 egg and chill.
2. Cut into cubes enough cold roast beef to yield 3 cups.
3. Drizzle meat broth over beef mixing to coat cubes
4. Set in refrigerator to chill.
5. Cut the hard-cooked egg into halves. Chop the egg white and set aside.
6. For Dressing – Mash the egg yolk with a fork or force through ricer or sieve. Mix in 1 uncooked egg yolk, cider vinegar and dry mustard, in order.
7. Add salad oil very gradually while beating constantly.
8. Mix in parsley, fillets, capers and thyme.
9. Pour dressing over beef and toss lightly to mix thoroughly. Garnish with the chopped egg white.

Prepare Quick Broth – dissolve in 1 cup hot water, 1 chicken bouillon cube for chicken broth or 1 beef bouillon cube (or ½ teaspoon concentrated meat extract) for meat broth.

Oriental Salad

ABOUT
8 SERVINGS

1½ cups strips of cold roast
  pork
2 cups sliced Chinese cabbage
  (celery cabbage)
1 16-oz. can bean sprouts
  (about 2 cups, drained)
1 5-oz. can water chestnuts
1¾ cups cooked rice
1 cup cooked peas
⅔ cup thick sour cream
⅓ cup mayonnaise
2 tablespoons soy sauce
1 tablespoon cider vinegar
1 teaspoon celery seed
¼ teaspoon garlic salt
¼ teaspoon pepper

1. Cut into thin strips enough cold roast pork to yield 1½ cups.
2. Wash, trim off roots, separate stalks, remove any blemishes and slice enough Chinese cabbage to yield 2 cups.
3. Drain contents of can of bean sprouts and can of water chestnuts.
4. Slice the water chestnuts. Combine the Chinese cabbage, pork, bean sprouts, water chestnuts, rice and peas.
5. Toss lightly to mix. Chill thoroughly in refrigerator.
6. Blend together and chill thoroughly sour cream, mayonnaise, soy sauce, cider vinegar, celery seed, garlic salt and pepper.
7. Just before serving, pour dressing over salad and toss lightly to mix thoroughly. Serve in a salad bowl; garnish with pimiento strips or green pepper strips.

Shrimp Salad

6 SERVINGS

1½ cups cooked shrimp,
  sliced in half lengthwise
½ cup diced cooked potatoes
2 hard-cooked eggs, sliced
½ cup chopped celery
¼ cup chopped green onions
½ cup mayonnaise or salad
  dressing
½ cup sour cream
½ teaspoon chili powder
Salt to taste
Lettuce leaves
Lemon wedges

1. Combine all ingredients, except lettuce and lemon wedges, and stir gently until evenly mixed and coated with dressing.
2. Refrigerate at least 1 hour before serving.
3. When ready to serve, place on lettuce leaves. Serve with lemon wedges.

Note: Shrimp salad also makes a delicious avocado filling.

Sea Garden Salad

SERVES 6 TO 8

1 pound fillet of halibut
1 6-ounce package lime gelatin
3 cups hot water
1 cup pineapple juice
2 tablespoons lime juice
1 cup diced canned pineapple
½ cup seedless white grapes
  (optional)
1 cup diced melon

1. Poach fish in water to cover about 10 minutes or just until done. Drain and cool.
2. Using a fork, separate into small chunks.
3. Dissolve gelatin in hot water; add pineapple juice and lime juice. Chill until consistency of unbeaten egg white.
4. Fold in fruits and fish. Turn into lightly oiled 2-quart mold.
5. Chill until firm.
6. Unmold on salad greens. Serve with mayonnaise.

Smorgasbord Pear Salads

12 SALADS

6 fresh Bartlett pears
Shrimp Filling
Zippy Cheese Filling
Celery-Olive Filling
Salad Greens

1. Halve and core pears. Fill 4 halves with Shrimp Filling, 4 with Zippy Cheese Filling, and 4 with Celery-Olive Filling.
2. Arrange filled pear halves on salad greens in a large shallow bowl or on a serving platter.

Shrimp Filling: Chop **1 cup cooked deveined shrimp** and combine with **¼ cup chopped celery, 2 tablespoons chopped parsley, 2 teaspoons instant minced onion, ½ teaspoon salt,** and **⅓ cup mayonnaise.**

Zippy Cheese Filling: Combine **1 cup cottage cheese, 1 tablespoon drained capers,** and **1 tablespoon chopped pimento-stuffed olives.**

Celery-Olive Filling: Combine in a small bowl **1 cup cooked sliced celery, ¼ cup ripe olives,** cut in wedges, and **1 tablespoon diced pimento.** Put into a jar with a lid **⅓ cup salad oil, 2 tablespoons vinegar, ½ teaspoon salt,** and **1½ teaspoons sugar;** cover and shake to blend. Pour over celery mixture. Let marinate 2 hours, stirring occasionally.

Smogasbord Pear Salads

Shrimp
and
Avocado
Salad

Shrimp and Avocado Salad

ABOUT
8 SERVINGS

1 cup wine vinegar
⅓ cup water
½ cup lemon juice
1 cup salad oil
¼ cup chopped parsley
2 cloves garlic, minced
1 tablespoon salt
¼ teaspoon freshly ground
 black pepper
1 tablespoon sugar
1 teaspoon dry mustard
1 teaspoon thyme, crushed
1 teaspoon oregano, crushed
2 pounds large cooked
 shrimp, peeled and
 deveined
3 small onions, sliced
⅓ cup chopped green pepper
2 ripe avocados, peeled and
 sliced

1. For marinade, combine vinegar, water, lemon juice, oil, parsley, and garlic in a bowl or a screwtop jar. Add a mixture of salt, pepper, sugar, dry mustard, thyme, and oregano; blend thoroughly.
2. Put shrimp, onions, and green pepper into a large shallow dish. Pour marinade over all, cover and refrigerate 8 hours or overnight.
3. About 1 hour before serving, put avocado slices into bowl. Pour enough marinade from shrimp over the avocado to cover completely.
4. To serve, remove avocado slices and shrimp from marinade and arrange on crisp **lettuce** in a large serving bowl.

Scallop Salad

SERVES 6

1 pound scallops
1 quart boiling water
1 teaspoon salt
1 small onion
½ clove garlic
½ cup French dressing
1½ cups chopped celery
½ cup diced sweet pickles
¼ cup mayonnaise
Lettuce

1. Drain and rinse scallops.
2. Drop into boiling water and add salt, onion and garlic.
3. Cook for 10 minutes.
4. Drain and chill.
5. Dice scallops and marinate in French dressing for 1 hour.
6. Combine with celery, pickles and mayonnaise and serve on crisp lettuce.
7. Garnish with cucumber slices.

Sea Food Medley

ABOUT
12 SERVINGS

1 6½-oz. can crab meat (about
1⅓ cups, drained)
2 6-oz. cans lobster meat (about
1½ cups, drained)
1 5-oz. can shrimp (about ¾
cup, drained; remove black
veins if present)
3 eggs
1 qt. (about ½ head) shredded
lettuce
1 cup diced celery
¼ cup sliced radishes
¼ cup sliced green onions
1 medium-size ripe avocado
2 tablespoons lemon juice
½ cup (about 2 oz.) walnuts
2 medium-size tomatoes, chilled
1 cup mayonnaise
¼ cup cream
1 teaspoon salt
¼ teaspoon pepper

1. Drain, remove and discard bony tissue, and separate contents of can of crab meat.
2. Drain contents of cans of lobster meat and shrimp.
3. Cut lobster and shrimp into pieces. Combine in a bowl with crab meat and chill in refrigerator.
4. Hard-cook eggs and chill.
5. Prepare and put lettuce, celery, radishes and onions into a large salad bowl.
6. Set in refrigerator to chill at least 1 hr.
7. Shortly before serving, prepare avocado and cut into cubes.
8. Coat pieces with lemon juice.
9. Add to the salad bowl. Dice the hard-cooked eggs and add to the salad bowl, together with the sea food. Coarsely chop and add walnuts.
10. Rinse, cut out stem ends, dice and add tomatoes.
11. Mix all ingredients together lightly but thoroughly.
12. Blend together mayonnaise, cream, salt and pepper.
13. Add to salad bowl and toss lightly.

Note: If desired, reserve lobster meat from claws or use some shrimp to garnish. Or top with **capers, green pepper strips** or **ripe olives.**

Kippered Herring Salad

SERVES 6

1 14-ounce can kippered
herring
2½ cups diced cooked beets
1 small onion, thinly sliced
¼ cup French dressing
1 small head lettuce
6 deviled eggs

1. Remove bone and skin from herring and break into large pieces.
2. Drain beets and add to herring.
3. Separate slices of onion into rings and add to beets.
4. Sprinkle with French dressing and chill for 1 hour.
5. Shred lettuce and arrange on salad plate.
6. Place salad in a mound on lettuce and arrange deviled eggs around it.

Herring Salad

10 TO 12
SERVINGS

2 qts. cold water
1 salt herring, cleaned and cut
into fillets
½ lb. boneless veal for stew,
cut in ½-inch cubes
3 cups water
1 lb. (about 5) medium-size
beets
2 small (about ½ lb.) potatoes
3 eggs
2 medium-size onions
1 large apple, rinsed and diced
1½ tablespoons white vinegar
½ teaspoon sugar
½ teaspoon salt
Few grains pepper
1 cup chilled whipping cream

1. Pour 2 qts. cold water into a large bowl.
2. Put herring into the water.
3. Set aside to soak 3 hrs.
4. **To Prepare Herring** – With a sharp knife cut off and discard head. Slit along underside of the fish from head to tail. Remove entrails and scrape insides well. Cut off tail and fins. Rinse thoroughly in cold water. Cut off a strip about ½ in. wide along each of cut edges. Discard strips. Make a slit along backbone just to the bone. Using a sharp knife, carefully pull and scrape the blue skin from the flesh. Be careful not to tear fish. Then cut along backbone through bone and flesh to remove one side of fish. Repeat for the second side. Remove as many of the small bones as possible without tearing fish.
5. **For Salad** – Set out veal for stew.
6. Put 3 cups water into a saucepan.

7.   Cook over medium heat about 1 hr., or until meat is tender. Drain; chill in refrigerator.

8.   Meanwhile, leaving on 1- 2-in. stem and the root end, cut off leaves from beets.

9.   Scrub beets thoroughly. Cook 30 to 45 min., or until just tender. When beets are tender, drain. Plunge beets into running cold water; peel off and discard skin, stem and root end. Cut beets into slices 1/4 in. thick. Cut slices into strips 1/4 in. wide. Set in refrigerator to chill.

10.   While beets cook, wash and scrub potatoes with a vegetable brush.

11.   Cook about 20 min., or until the potatoes are tender when pierced with a fork. Drain potatoes. To dry potatoes, shake pan over low heat. Peel potatoes and dice. Chill in refrigerator.

12.   Hard-cook eggs.

13.   Cut 2 of the peeled eggs into halves lengthwise. Finely chop the egg whites and egg yolks separately and set aside. Cut the remaining peeled egg into slices crosswise. Set aside.

14.   Put a bowl and beater in refrigerator to chill.

15.   Clean onions and finely chop.

16.   Drain the herring, dry on absorbent paper, and cut into 1/2-to-3/4-in. pieces. Put the herring, veal, potatoes, and onion into a large bowl with apple.

17.   Pour over ingredients in bowl and mixture of white vinegar, sugar, salt and pepper.

18.   Toss lightly to coat evenly.

19.   Using the chilled bowl and beater, beat whipping cream until cream is of medium consistency (piles softly).

20.   Turn the whipped cream over the herring mixture and toss lightly until thoroughly combined. Add the beets and mix thoroughly, being careful not to break the strips. Turn into a serving bowl and chill thoroughly in refrigerator. If desired, turn Herring Salad into a 2-qt. mold. Pack lightly. Chill thoroughly.

21.   When ready to serve, spoon the chopped egg white around the edge of the salad, the chopped egg yolk over the center. Arrange the hard-cooked egg slices in a circle between the chopped egg white and egg yolks. Complete the garnish with sprigs of **parsley.** Place a cruet of **white vinegar,** colored with beet juice, and a cruet of **cream** on the table so that each person may sour the salad to his own taste.

Pickled Herring

SERVES 4

1 salt herring
1/3 cup vinegar
1/2 small onion
1 teaspoon mixed pickling
    spices

1.   Soak herring in cold water overnight.

2.   Clean, removing skin and bones.

3.   Cut into 1-inch pieces and place in jar or bowl; add vinegar, onion and spices.

4.   Let stand several hours before serving.

Haitian Rock Lobster Salad

8 SERVINGS

8 rock lobster tails
Court Bouillon for Fish and Shellfish (page 76)
4 cups rice
16 cherry tomatoes, washed and stemmed
1 cup cubed pared cucumber
3 celery stalks, diced
1 cup cubed fresh pineapple
1 cup small Greek black olives
¼ cup capers
1 cup French Dressing Antillaise for Salads (page 72)
4 hard-cooked eggs, peeled and quartered
¾ cup amber rum

1. Simmer lobster tails in court bouillon 20 minutes. Belly side down on a board, split the tail lengthwise with a sharp knife and keep warm in the bouillon until serving time (see Note).
2. Toss rice with vegetables, pineapple, olives, and capers. Add dressing and toss again.
3. Mound the rice mixture on a large silver platter, garnish with hard-cooked egg quarters, and edge platter with drained cooked lobster tails.
4. At the table, warm rum, ignite it, and pour it flaming over the lobster.

Note: If you have room in the freezer, save the court bouillon to use as a base for Béchamel Sauce for fish or for a chowder.

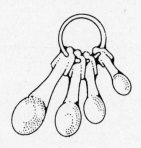

Luscious Rock Lobster Salad

6 SERVINGS

3 6- to 8-ounce frozen rock lobster tails (or use 3 6-ounce cans rock lobster meat)
1½ quarts water
1½ teaspoons salt
1 cup diced celery
½ cup slivered unblanched almonds
1 tablespoon minced scallions or onion
¾ cup mayonnaise
2 tablespoons cream
2 tablespoons lemon juice
¼ teaspoon sugar
¼ teaspoon salt
¼ teaspoon crushed dried tarragon leaves
⅛ teaspoon white pepper

1. If using canned rock lobster, chill in the can in refrigerator. Drain and cut into chunks when ready to prepare salad.
2. To Cook Frozen Rock Lobster Tails – Bring water and salt to boiling in a heavy sauce pot or kettle.
3. Add frozen or thawed rock lobster tails to kettle. Cover; bring water again to boiling, reduce heat and simmer for 7 to 12 minutes.
4. Drain tails, cover with cold water and drain again. Using scissors or a sharp knife, cut through thin shell or underside of each tail. Insert fingers under meat and carefully pull it out. Cool meat; chill in refrigerator. Cut into chunks when ready to prepare salad.
5. To Complete Salad – Prepare celery, almonds and minced scallions or onion.
6. Put into a large bowl, reserving about 2 tablespoons of the almonds for garnish. Add the rock lobster meat.
7. Blend together mayonnaise, cream, lemon juice, sugar, ¼ teaspoon salt, tarragon leaves and white pepper.
8. Add to the ingredients in the bowl, toss lightly to mix thoroughly. Chill.
9. Serve in a chilled salad bowl; garnish with reserved almonds and **ripe olives.**

Haitian Rock Lobster Salad

Lobster Salad

ABOUT
12 SERVINGS

6 cups diced fresh lobster
  meat, chilled
3 hard-cooked eggs, mashed
  through a sieve
1 large scallion, minced
1 small leek, finely chopped
2 teaspoons tarragon
½ teaspoon thyme
2 garlic cloves, crushed in a
  garlic press
2 cups mayonnaise
1 tablespoon capers
Juice of 1 lemon
Cucumber, sliced paper thin
Tomato wedges for garnish

1. Combine all ingredients except cucumber and tomato. Adjust seasoning.
2. Spoon into heated **pastry shells,** a **lobster** cavity, or on a bed of **lettuce.** Garnish with cucumber slices and tomato wedges.

Avocado Crab Salad, Paella Style

6 TO 8
SERVINGS

2 cans (5 oz. each) lobster (or
  use fresh lobster)
2 doz. small clams*
¾ lb. fresh shrimp
1 clove garlic, crushed
1 tablespoon butter or
  margarine
2 tablespoons dry sherry
¼ teaspoon saffron, crushed
Dash pepper
1¼ cups uncooked rice
¾ cup small pimiento-stuffed
  olives
2 ripe avocados

1. Drain and remove bones from lobster (*see* note below).
2. Cook clams gently in boiling salted water to cover until the shells open.
3. Remove clams and cook shrimp, in the same liquid 3 to 5 min., covered.
4. Chill the shellfish, strain and measure 2½ cups of the fish broth into a medium saucepan. Add garlic, butter or margarine, dry sherry, saffron, and pepper.
5. Bring to boiling and add uncooked rice.
6. Cover and cook over low heat about 15 min., or until rice kernels are soft and broth is absorbed.
7. Shell the chilled shrimp. (If using freshly cooked lobster, shell and cut meat into pieces; reserve 2 claws for garnish.)
8. Combine rice, clams, shrimp and lobster in a large mixing bowl. Add pimiento-stuffed olives.
9. Mix lightly with a fork and chill thoroughly.
10. When ready to serve avocados, peel, halve, remove seeds and brush lightly with lemon juice.
11. Turn salad mixture into serving bowl and arrange avocado, cut in wedges, over top. (Garnish with lobster claws, if available.)
12. Serve the salad with **olive oil, herbed mayonnaise, salad dressing** or **tartar sauce,** as desired.

Note: If using fresh lobster meat, cook lobsters (about 1¼ lbs. each) in 3 qts. boiling water and 3 tablespoons salt. Cover pot and cook lobsters over low heat about 20 min. Remove lobsters and use the same liquid to cook the clams and shrimp (one shellfish at a time). Reserve the cooking liquid.

* If desired, 1 doz. mussels may be substituted for 1 doz. small clams.

Avocado Crab Salad, Paella Style

Shrimp Salad with Coral Dressing

Shrimp Salad with Coral Dressing

6 SERVINGS

2 cups cooked, peeled, and
   deveined shrimp
1½ cups cooked rice
½ cup sliced celery
½ cup chopped unpeeled
   cucumbers
¼ cup chopped chives
⅓ cup mayonnaise
¼ cup dairy sour cream
1 tablespoon chili sauce
¼ teaspoon onion salt
⅛ teaspoon pepper
1½ teaspoons tarragon vinegar
Salad greens
Horseradish (optional)
Lemon wedges

1. Toss shrimp, rice, celery, cucumbers, and chives together.
2. Blend ingredients for dressing. Pour over shrimp mixture and toss thoroughly. Chill.
3. Serve on salad greens. Top with a little horseradish, if desired, and garnish with lemon wedges.
4. Accompany with champagne.

Tuna Salad

ABOUT
4 SERVINGS

2 7-oz. cans tuna (about 2 cups,
   drained)
1 cup sliced celery
¼ cup sliced radishes
2 tablespoons chopped green
   pepper
½ cup salad dressing
1 tablespoon lemon juice
1 tablespoon minced onion
¼ teaspoon pepper
Crisp salad greens

1. Drain tuna well and separate into small chunks and put into a bowl.
2. Prepare celery, radishes and green pepper and mix lightly with the tuna.
3. Blend together and add salad dressing, lemon juice, onion and pepper.
4. Toss lightly to mix thoroughly.
5. Chill mixture thoroughly in refrigerator.
6. To serve, arrange crisp salad greens on a chilled serving plate or in a salad bowl.
7. Spoon the tuna salad in the center. Garnish with strips of **pimiento.**

Tuna-Cheese Salad: Follow recipe for Tuna Salad. Omit celery and radishes. Toss tuna lightly with 1½ cups (about 6 oz.) shredded **Swiss cheese.** Increase salad dressing to about 1 cup. Before serving, add ⅔ cup coarsely chopped **cashew nuts** and mix lightly.

Tuna Salad Piquant: Follow recipe for Tuna Salad. Omit celery, radishes and onion. Toss tuna lightly with ½ cup small white **cocktail onions.** Blend ¼ cup **chili sauce** with salad dressing mixture.

Tuna-Apple Salad: Follow recipe for Tuna Salad. Omit radishes and salad dressing mixture. Mix 2 cups (about 2 medium size) diced red **apple,** unpared, with the tuna. Toss salad lightly with about ⅔ cup **Curry** and **Mayonnaise.**

Tuna Salad in Tomatoes

SERVES 4

1 7-ounce can tuna
½ cup chopped celery
2 sour pickles, chopped
1 hard-cooked egg, chopped
2 tablespoons French dressing
4 tomatoes
Salt
⅓ cup mayonnaise
1 head lettuce

1. Flake tuna and combine with celery, pickle and egg.
2. Marinate in French dressing and chill.
3. Peel tomatoes, scoop out centers, sprinkle with salt, invert and chill.
4. Combine chopped center of tomatoes with tuna mixture and mayonnaise, stuff tomatoes with mixture.
5. Serve on lettuce.
6. Garnish if desired with quartered hard-cooked eggs and ripe olives.

Rice Salad with Assorted Sausages

6 TO 8
SERVINGS

⅓ cup white wine vinegar
1 teaspoon lemon juice
¼ teaspoon French mustard
1 teaspoon salt
¼ teaspoon ground black pepper
⅓ cup salad oil
3 cups cooked enriched white rice, cooled
3 cups finely shredded red cabbage
½ cup raisins
½ cup walnut pieces
Greens
Link sausage (such as bratwurst, smoky links, and frankfurters), cooked

1. Put vinegar into a bottle. Add lemon juice, mustard, salt, and pepper. Cover and shake. Add oil and shake well.
2. Combine rice, cabbage, raisins, and walnuts in a bowl; chill.
3. When ready to serve, shake dressing well and pour over salad; toss until well mixed.
4. Arrange greens on luncheon plates, spoon salad on greens, and accompany with assorted sausages.

Curried Breast of Chicken Salad

6 SERVINGS

6 cups bite-size pieces cooked chicken
1½ cups sliced celery
1 can (8½ ounces) water chestnuts, drained and cut in thirds
½ teaspoon salt
¼ teaspoon finely ground pepper
1 cup Mock Mayonnaise (page 78)
1 teaspoon curry powder
2 tablespoons dry sherry
Lettuce leaves
Orange slices

1. Combine chicken, celery, water chestnuts, salt, and pepper.
2. Mix Mock Mayonnaise, curry, and sherry; stir gently into chicken mixture. Serve on lettuce-lined plates; garnish with orange slices.

Stewed Chicken

ABOUT
3 TO 3½ CUPS
DICED CHICKEN

1 stewing chicken, 4 to 5 lbs.
   ready-to-cook weight
Hot water to barely cover
1 small onion
3 sprigs parsley
2 3-in. pieces celery with leaves
1 bay leaf
3 peppercorns
2 teaspoons salt

1. Set out a kettle or sauce pot having a tight-fitting cover.
2. Clean chicken. (If chicken is frozen, thaw according to directions on package.)
3. Disjoint and cut into serving-size pieces. Rinse chicken pieces and giblets. Refrigerate the liver. Put chicken pieces, gizzard, heart and neck into the kettle and add hot water to barely cover.
4. Add to water onion, parsley, celery with leaves, bay leaf, peppercorns and salt.
5. Bring water to boiling; remove foam. Cover kettle tightly, reduce heat and simmer chicken 1 hr., skimming foam from surface as necessary. Continue cooking chicken 1 to 2 hrs. longer, or until thickest pieces are tender when pierced with a fork. During last 15 min. of cooking time, add liver to kettle.
6. Remove chicken and giblets from broth. Cool chicken slightly and remove skin. Remove meat from bones. Cut meat into pieces as directed in recipes. Strain broth and cool slightly. Remove fat that rises to surface. Refrigerate fat and broth and use in other food preparation. Unless using meat immediately, cool, cover and refrigerate.

Chicken Salad De Luxe

ABOUT
6 SERVINGS

3 cups cooked chicken cubes
   (see Stewed Chicken, above)
1 cup diced celery
½ cup small seedless grapes (or
   use green grapes cut into
   halves and seeded)
½ cup (2 to 3 oz.) toasted
   pecans or toasted blanched
   almonds, chopped
¼ cup (1 oz.) moist shredded
   coconut, cut fine
¼ cup chilled whipping cream
¾ cup Cooked Salad Dressing
   (page 75)

1. Set a small bowl and rotary beater in refrigerator to chill.
2. Prepare and put chicken cubes and celery into a large bowl.
3. Rinse grapes, drain, and add to bowl.
4. Set in refrigerator to chill.
5. Prepare pecans or coconut and set aside.
6. Before serving, using chilled bowl and beater, beat whipping cream until of medium consistency (piles softly).
7. Blend the whipped cream into ¾ cup Cooked Salad Dressing.
8. Lightly toss nuts and coconut with chicken mixture. Add salad dressing mixture; toss gently to coat evenly.

Chicken-Curry Salad: Follow recipe for Chicken De Luxe. Blend ½ to 1 teaspoon **curry powder** into the salad dressing mixture.

Chicken-Roquefort Salad: Follow recipe for Chicken Salad De Luxe. Substitute 2 cups shredded **lettuce** for celery. Omit grapes and coconut. Increase salad dressing to 1 cup and blend in 1½ oz. **Roquefort cheese,** crumbled.

Turkey Salad: Follow recipe for Chicken Salad De Luxe or any variation. Substitute cooked **turkey** for chicken.

Macaroni Picnic Salad

Macaroni Picnic Salad

ABOUT
8 SERVINGS

1 package (16 ounce) elbow
   macaroni (4 cups)
1 cup each sliced radishes,
   sliced celery and sliced
   sweet gherkins
2 tablespoons chopped onion
1 cup mayonnaise
⅓ cup sweet pickle liquid
¼ cup spicy brown mustard
1 teaspoon prepared
   horseradish
1 teaspoon salt
⅛ teaspoon white pepper

1. Cook macaroni in boiling salted water following directions on package.
2. Drain in colander.
3. Combine the macaroni in a large bowl with radishes, celery, sweet gherkins and chopped onion.
4. Mix mayonnaise, sweet pickle liquid, brown mustard, horseradish, salt, and white pepper thoroughly in a small bowl.
5. Toss dressing with macaroni mixture. Chill.
6. When ready to serve salad, garnish with **salad greens, radish roses** and **gherkin fans.**

Molded Salads

Stewed Tomato Aspic

4 TO 6
SERVINGS

1 envelope unflavored gelatin
½ cup cold water
1 can (16 ounces) stewed
  tomatoes
1 tablespoon sugar
¼ teaspoon salt
1 tablespoon cider vinegar
1½ teaspoons prepared
  horseradish
1½ teaspoons grated onion
¼ teaspoon Worcestershire
  sauce
2 hard-cooked eggs, cut in
  quarters
Salad greens

1. Sprinkle gelatin over water to soften.
2. Turn tomatoes into a saucepan and break up any large pieces with a spoon. Stir in sugar, salt, vinegar, horseradish, onion, and Worcestershire sauce and heat to boiling. Add softened gelatin and stir until dissolved.
3. Chill gelatin until slightly thickened.
4. Arrange egg quarters around bottom of a 3- or 4-cup mold. Spoon slightly thickened gelatin mixture into mold. Chill until firm.
5. Unmold and garnish with crisp greens.

Tomato Aspic

6 TO 8
SERVINGS

4 cups tomato juice
⅓ cup chopped celery leaves
⅓ cup chopped onion
2½ tablespoons sugar
1¼ teaspoons salt
1 bay leaf
½ cup cold water
2 envelopes unflavored
  gelatin
2½ tablespoons cider vinegar

1. Set out a 1-quart mold.
2. Pour tomato juice into a saucepan.
3. Add celery leaves, onion, sugar, salt and bay leaf to tomato juice.
4. Simmer, uncovered 10 minutes, stirring occasionally.
5. Meanwhile, pour water into a small bowl.
6. Sprinkle gelatin evenly over water.
7. Let stand until softened.
8. Lightly oil the mold with salad or cooking oil (not olive oil); set aside to drain.
9. Remove tomato juice mixture from heat and strain into a large bowl. Immediately add the softened gelatin to hot tomato juice mixture and stir until gelatin is completely dissolved.
10. Add cider vinegar and stir well.
11. Pour tomato-juice mixture into the prepared mold. Cool; chill in refrigerator until firm.
12. Unmold onto chilled serving plate.

Tomato Aspic

Tomato Aspic – Cream Cheese Salad Ring

ABOUT
24 SERVINGS

Tomato Aspic Ring
Cream Cheese Ring
Salad dressing
4 cups tomato juice
¹⁄₃ cup chopped celery leaves
¹⁄₃ cup chopped onion
2¹⁄₂ tablespoons sugar
1¹⁄₂ teaspoons salt
¹⁄₂ bay leaf
¹⁄₂ cup cold water
2 env. unflavored gelatin
2¹⁄₂ tablespoons cider vinegar
¹⁄₂ cup cold water
1 env. unflavored gelatin
9 oz. cream cheese
2 cups thick sour cream
4 teaspoons lemon juice
1¹⁄₂ tablespoons sugar
1 teaspoon salt

1. Two identical 1-qt. ring molds will be needed.
2. For Salad Ring – Prepare and chill until firm Tomato Aspic Ring and Cream Cheese Ring.
3. When ready for serving, unmold the Tomato Aspic Ring onto a chilled plate large enough for the aspic to be expanded to twice its size. Cut aspic into 1-in. slices and spread slices about 1-in. apart.
4. Unmold Cream Cheese Ring onto a second chilled plate. Cut into 1-in. slices. Transfer slices to the alternating spaces between the tomato aspic slices. Arrange so that a perfect ring is formed again.
5. Place on plate in the center of salad ring a small bowl of salad dressing.
6. For Tomato Aspic Ring – Pour tomato juice into a saucepan.
7. Add to tomato juice celery leaves, onion, 2¹⁄₂ tablespoons sugar, 1¹⁄₂ teaspoons salt and bay leaf.
8. Simmer uncovered, 10 min.
9. Meanwhile, pour ¹⁄₂ cup cold water into a small bowl.
10. Sprinkle unflavored gelatin evenly over cold water.
11. Set aside.
12. Lightly oil one ring mold with salad or cooking oil (not olive oil). Set it aside to drain.
13. Remove tomato juice mixture from heat. Strain liquid into a large bowl. Immediately add the softened gelatin to tomato juice mixture and stir until gelatin is completely dissolved. Add cider vinegar and stir well.
14. Pour mixture into the prepared mold. Cool and place in refrigerator to chill until firm.
15. For Cream Cheese Ring – Lightly oil the second mold with salad or cooking oil (not olive oil). Set it aside to drain.
16. Pour ¹⁄₂ cup cold water into a small saucepan.
17. Sprinkle 1 env. unflavored gelatin evenly over cold water.
18. Set the saucepan over low heat and stir constantly until gelatin is completely dissolved. Remove from heat.
19. Beat cream cheese until very soft.
20. Mix in sour cream, lemon juice, 1¹⁄₂ tablespoons sugar, and 1 teaspoon salt in order (adding cream gradually and stirring until smooth after each addition).
21. Blend dissolved gelatin into cream cheese mixture. Turn mixture into the prepared mold. Place in refrigerator to chill until firm.

Tomato Aspic Squares: Follow recipe for Tomato Aspic-Cream Cheese Salad Ring. Omit salad ring and Cream Cheese Ring. Set out a 13x9x2-in. pan. Pour **Tomato Aspic** into pan, cool and chill in refrigerator until firm. When ready to serve, cut into 2-in. squares. Beat 1¹⁄₂ oz. (¹⁄₂ pkg.) **cream cheese,** softened, and 1 tablespoon **milk** until fluffy. Force cream cheese through a pastry bag and No. 27 decorating tube onto center of each square. Arrange squares on a serving tray and garnish with sprigs of parsley.
ABOUT 2 DOZ. ASPIC SQUARES

Beermato Aspic

Beermato Aspic

8 SERVINGS

1 can (18 ounces) tomato
  juice (2¼ cups)
1 can or bottle (12 ounces)
  beer
⅓ cup chopped onion
⅓ cup chopped celery leaves
  (optional)
2½ tablespoons sugar
1 tablespoon lemon juice
½ teaspoon salt
1 bay leaf
2 envelopes unflavored
  gelatin
¼ cup cold water

1. Combine tomato juice (reserve ¼ cup), beer, onion, celery leaves, sugar, lemon juice, salt, and bay leaf in a saucepan. Simmer, uncovered, 10 minutes.
2. Meanwhile, sprinkle gelatin over cold water and reserved tomato juice in a large bowl; let stand to soften.
3. Strain hot tomato juice mixture into bowl; stir until gelatin is completely dissolved.
4. Pour into a lightly oiled 1-quart mold. Chill until firm. Unmold onto crisp **salad greens.**

Note: For individual aspics, turn mixture into 8 oiled ½-cup molds. Chill until firm.

Chicken-Tomato Aspic Ring

8 TO 10
SERVINGS

2 cups tomato juice
3 tablespoons chopped onion
½ teaspoon salt
⅛ teaspoon pepper
2 or 3 drops Tabasco
1 3-oz. pkg. lemon-flavored gelatin
⅔ cup packaged pre-cooked rice
1 cup chopped cooked chicken (see Stewed Chicken, page 47)
½ cup chopped celery
¼ cup chopped stuffed olives
¼ cup cold water
1 env. unflavored gelatin
1 cup mayonnaise
½ cup cream
½ teaspoon salt
¼ teaspoon paprika
⅛ teaspoon pepper
⅛ teaspoon crushed dried tarragon leaves

1. Lightly oil a 1½-qt. ring mold with salad or cooking oil (not olive oil); set aside to drain.
2. For Tomato Aspic Layer – Pour tomato juice into a saucepan.
3. Add to tomato juice onion, ½ teaspoon salt, ⅛ teaspoon pepper and Tabasco.
4. Simmer, uncovered, 10 min.
5. Meanwhile, empty gelatin into a bowl.
6. Remove tomato juice mixture from heat. Strain into the bowl with gelatin and stir until gelatin is completely dissolved.
7. Pour into the prepared mold. Cool; chill in refrigerator until partially set.
8. For Chicken-Rice Layer – Meanwhile, cook rice according to directions on package.
9. Turn rice into a large bowl; let stand until cooled.
10. Chop and set aside enough cooked chicken to yield 1 cup.
11. Prepare celery and olives.
12. Pour water into a small cup or custard cup.
13. Sprinkle 1 env. unflavored gelatin evenly over water.
14. Let stand until softened. Dissolve completely by placing cup over very hot water. Stir gelatin and blend into a mixture of mayonnaise, cream, ½ teaspoon salt, paprika, ⅛ teaspoon pepper and tarragon leaves.
15. Add the chopped chicken, celery, olives and the mayonnaise mixture to bowl containing cooled rice; mix thoroughly.
16. When first layer in mold is partially set, immediately spoon the chicken-rice mixture into the mold. (Both layers should be of almost the same consistency when combined to avoid separation when unmolded). Chill in refrigerator until firm.
17. Unmold onto chilled serving plate.

Turkey-Tomato Aspic Ring: Follow recipe for Chicken-Tomato Aspic Ring. Subsitute cooked **turkey** for the chicken.

Avocado-Tomato Aspic Ring: Follow recipe for Chicken-Tomato Aspic Ring. For Tomato Aspic only: use a 1-qt. mold. Add 3 tablespoons chopped **celery leaves,** 1 tablespoon **sugar** and ½ **bay leaf** to tomato juice mixture before heating. Substitute **strawberry-flavored gelatin** for lemon-flavored gelatin and add 1 tablespoon **lemon juice.** Cool; chill until gelatin mixture is slightly thicker than consistency of thick, unbeaten egg white. Meanwhile prepare 1½ cups diced **avocado.** When gelatin mixture is of desired consistency, mix in the diced avocado. Turn into the prepared mold and chill in refrigerator until firm.

Chicken Mousse Amandine

8 SERVINGS

½ cup dry white wine, such as sauterne
2 envelopes unflavored gelatin
3 egg yolks
1 cup milk
1 cup chicken broth
½ cup (about 3 ounces) almonds, finely chopped
3 cups ground cooked chicken
¼ cup mayonnaise
2 tablespoons minced parsley
2 tablespoons chopped green olives
1 teaspoon lemon juice
1 teaspoon onion juice
½ teaspoon salt
½ teaspoon celery salt
Few grains paprika
Few grains cayenne pepper
½ cup chilled heavy cream
Sprigs of parsley

1. Place a small bowl and a rotary beater in refrigerator to chill.
2. Pour wine into a small cup and sprinkle gelatin evenly over wine; set aside.
3. Beat egg yolks slightly in top of a double boiler; add milk gradually, stirring constantly.
4. Stir in the chicken broth gradually. Cook over simmering water, stirring constantly and rapidly until mixture coats a metal spoon.
5. Remove from heat. Stir softened gelatin and immediately stir it into the hot mixture until gelatin is completely dissolved. Cool; chill in refrigerator or over ice and water until gelatin mixture begins to gel (becomes slightly thicker). If mixture is placed over ice and water, stir frequently; if placed in refrigerator, stir occasionally.
6. Blend almonds and chicken into chilled custard mixture along with mayonnaise, parsley, olives, lemon juice, onion juice, and a mixture of salt, celery salt, paprika, and cayenne pepper.
7. Using the chilled bowl and beater, beat cream until of medium consistency (piles softly).
8. Fold whipped cream into chicken mixture. Turn into a 1½-quart fancy mold. Chill in refrigerator until firm.
9. Unmold onto chilled serving plate and, if desired, garnish with sprigs of parsley.

Dubonnet Chicken Salad Mold

ABOUT
10 SERVINGS

2 envelopes unflavored gelatin
1 cup cranberry juice cocktail
1 cup red Dubonnet
1 cup red currant syrup
1 envelope unflavored gelatin
¾ cup cold water
1 tablespoon soy sauce
1 cup mayonnaise
1½ cups finely diced cooked chicken
½ cup finely chopped celery
¼ cup toasted blanched almonds, finely chopped
½ cup whipping cream, whipped
Leaf lettuce
Cucumber slices, scored
Pitted ripe olives

1. Soften 2 envelopes gelatin in cranberry juice in a saucepan; set over low heat and stir until gelatin is dissolved. Remove from heat and stir in Dubonnet and currant syrup.
2. Pour into a 2-quart fancy tube mold. Chill until set but not firm.
3. Meanwhile, soften 1 envelope gelatin in cold water in a saucepan. Set over low heat and stir until gelatin is dissolved.
4. Remove from heat and stir in soy sauce and mayonnaise until thoroughly blended. Chill until mixture becomes slightly thicker. Mix in chicken, celery, and almonds. Fold in whipped cream until blended.
5. Spoon mixture into mold over first layer. Chill 8 hours or overnight.
6. Unmold onto a chilled serving plate. Garnish with lettuce, cucumber, and olives.

Chicken Salad Sensation

8 TO 10
SERVINGS

1 3-oz. pkg. lemon-flavored gelatin
1 cup very hot water
1 cup ginger ale
1 tablespoon lemon juice
1½ cups mayonnaise
2 cups cubed cooked chicken (see Stewed Chicken, page 47)
⅔ cup halved and seeded Tokay grapes
½ cup (about 3 oz.) chopped blanched almonds
⅓ cup chopped celery
⅓ cup chopped green pepper

1. Set out a 1½-qt. mold.
2. Empty gelatin into a bowl.
3. Add and stir water until gelatin is completely dissolved.
4. Blend in ginger ale and lemon juice.
5. Put mayonnaise into a large bowl.
6. Add the gelatin mixture gradually, stirring constantly until blended. Chill until mixture begins to gel (gets slightly thicker).
7. Lightly oil the mold with salad or cooking oil (not olive oil); set aside.
8. Prepare chicken, grapes, almonds, celery and green pepper and set aside.
9. When gelatin mixture is of desired consistency, stir in the chicken, grapes, almonds, celery and green pepper. Turn into the prepared mold and chill in refrigerator until firm.
10. Unmold onto chilled serving plate.

Ham Mousse

SERVES
8 TO 10

1 pound chopped ham
2 small chopped cucumbers
1 bunch chopped dill
1 cup heavy cream
2½ teaspoons prepared mustard
2 teaspoons unflavored gelatin
6 tablespoons cold water
2 tomatoes
1 frozen turkey roll (1 pound)
1 can white asparagus with tips (1 pound)
1 package frozen peas (cooked according to directions)
1 can creamed mushrooms (8 ounces)

1. Mix the chopped ham, cucumber and dill.
2. Beat the cream to a light foam and season with the mustard.
3. Melt the gelatin in ¼ cup cold water in a double boiler.
4. Stir the melted gelatin and the chopped ham into the cream. Pour into a water-rinsed ring mold, and place the mousse in the refrigerator to set.
5. Dip the tomatoes in hot water, remove the skin and cut them in halves.
6. Carve the turkey roll in even slices. Place the ham mousse in the middle of a large round dish. If the ring mold is dipped in hot water for a moment it will slide out easily. Put the asparagus in the middle of the mousse and arrange turkey slices in groups around the mousse. Surround with tomatoes and peas. Distribute the creamed mushrooms on the turkey slices.

Garden-Green Salad Mold

ABOUT
8 SERVINGS

1 package (3 ounces) lime-flavored gelatin
¼ teaspoon salt
1 cup boiling water
1 cup cold water
1 ripe medium avocado
1 tablespoon lemon juice
2 cups finely shredded cabbage
½ cup thinly sliced radishes
½ cup thinly sliced green onions with tops
Crisp greens

1. Put gelatin and salt into a bowl; add boiling water and stir until completely dissolved. Blend in cold water. Chill until slightly thickened.
2. Mash avocado and stir in lemon juice; blend thoroughly with gelatin. Mix in cabbage, radishes, and green onions.
3. Turn into a 1-quart mold or individual molds and chill until firm. Unmold onto chilled serving plate and garnish with salad greens.

Ham Mousse

Cucumber Mousse

4 TO 6
SERVINGS

1 package (3 ounces) lime-
flavored gelatin
¾ cup boiling water
1 cup cottage cheese
1 cup mayonnaise or salad
dressing
2 tablespoons grated onion
¾ cup grated cucumber
1 cup slivered almonds

1. Dissolve gelatin in boiling water. Stir in cottage cheese, mayonnaise, and onion until well blended. Fold in cucumber and almonds.
2. Pour mixture into a 1-quart mold. Refrigerate until set.

Molded Spinach Cottage Cheese on Platter

6 TO 8
SERVINGS

1 package (10 ounces) frozen
chopped spinach
2 envelopes unflavored
gelatin
¾ cup water
2 chicken bouillon cubes
2 tablespoons lemon juice
1½ cups creamed cottage
cheese
½ cup sour cream
½ cup sliced celery
⅓ cup chopped green pepper
2 tablespoons minced green
onion

1. Cook and drain spinach, reserving liquid. Add enough water to liquid to make ½ cup. Set spinach and liquid aside.
2. Soften gelatin in ¾ cup water in a saucepan; add bouillon cubes. Set over low heat; stirring occasionally, until gelatin and bouillon cubes are dissolved. Remove from heat; stir in spinach liquid and lemon juice. Set aside.
3. Beat cottage cheese until fairly smooth with mixer or in electric blender. Blend with sour cream and then gelatin mixture. Stir in spinach, celery, green pepper, and onion. Turn into a 5-cup mold. Chill until firm.
4. Unmold onto a chilled large platter. If desired, arrange slices of summer sausage around the mold.

Deviled Egg Salad

6 SERVINGS

6 eggs
½ cup cold water
1 env. unflavored gelatin
3 oz. (1 pkg.) cream cheese,
softened
½ cup mayonnaise
¼ cup ketchup
2 tablespoons cider vinegar
3 drops Tabasco
¼ cup finely chopped green
pepper
¼ cup finely chopped celery
2 tablespoons finely chopped
pimiento
1 tablespoon finely chopped
parsley
1 teaspoon grated onion
1 teaspoon salt

1. Hard-cook eggs and chill.
2. Meanwhile, lightly oil six ½-cup individual molds with salad or cooking oil (not olive oil); set aside to drain.
3. Pour water into a small cup or custard cup.
4. Sprinkle gelatin evenly over water.
5. Let stand until softened.
6. Meanwhile, beat together cream cheese, mayonnaise, ketchup, vinegar and Tabasco until fluffy.
7. Dissolve gelatin completely by placing cup over very hot water. Stir it and add gradually to the cream cheese mixture.
8. Chop the hard-cooked eggs. Add to the cream cheese mixture with green pepper, celery, pimiento, parsley, onion and salt.
9. Mix thoroughly. Turn into the prepared molds and chill in refrigerator until firm.
10. Unmold onto chilled serving plates. If desired, serve with slices of cold **ham;** garnish with **watercress.**

Egg Salad: Follow recipe for Deviled Egg Salad. Omit molds. Reserve 1 hard-cooked egg for garnish. Decrease mayonnaise to ¼ cup and ketchup to 2 tablespoons. Omit gelatin, cold water, vinegar and Tabasco. Spoon onto **Bibb lettuce leaves** and top each serving with a slice of egg. Or garnish each serving generously with minced **parsley** before topping with egg slice.

Tangy Cabbage Mold

6 SERVINGS

1 envelope unflavored gelatin
¼ cup cold water
¼ cup sugar
2 tablespoons lemon juice
½ teaspoon salt
1 can or bottle (12 ounces) beer
1½ cups shredded cabbage (about ¼ of a 2-pound head)
½ green pepper, shredded

1. Soften gelatin in cold water in a saucepan. Stir over low heat until dissolved.
2. Add sugar, lemon juice, and salt; stir until dissolved. Add beer. Chill until partially thickened.
3. Stir in cabbage and green pepper.
4. Turn into a 3½-cup mold, a shallow 1½-quart oblong casserole (8x6 inches), or 6 individual molds.

Mustard Relish Mold

ABOUT
12 SERVINGS

1 cup cold water
2 envelopes unflavored gelatin
6 eggs
1½ cups sugar
1½ tablespoons dry mustard
1¼ teaspoons salt
1½ cups vinegar
1 16-ounce can peas (about 1¾ cups, drained)
1 cup (about 2 medium-size) grated carrot
1 cup chopped celery
1 tablespoon minced parsley
Curly endive or other crisp greens

1. A 1½-quart mold will be needed.
2. Pour water into a small bowl.
3. Sprinkle gelatin evenly over cold water.
4. Let stand until softened.
5. Beat eggs slightly in top of a double boiler.
6. Blend in a mixture of sugar, mustard, and salt.
7. Add vinegar gradually, stirring constantly.
8. Cook over simmering water, stirring constantly, until mixture thickens. Remove from simmering water. Stir softened gelatin; add to egg mixture and stir until gelatin is completely dissolved. Cool, chill until mixture begins to gel (gets slightly thicker).
9. Meanwhile drain peas.
10. Lightly oil the mold with salad or cooking oil (not olive oil) and set it aside to drain.
11. Prepare carrot, celery, and parsley.
12. When gelatin is of desired consistency, blend in the vegetables. Turn into the prepared mold. Chill in refrigerator until firm.
13. Unmold onto chilled serving plate. Garnish with curly endive or other crisp greens.

Buffet Salmon Mousse

SERVES
8 TO 10

1 tablespoon unflavored gelatin
¼ cup cold water
2 tablespoons sugar
1 teaspoon salt
1 teaspoon prepared mustard
½ cup vinegar
2 egg yolks, beaten
1 tablespoon prepared horseradish
1 1-pound can salmon
1 cup chopped celery
½ cup heavy cream, whipped
Olives, sliced
Pimiento strips

1. Soften gelatin in cold water.
2. Mix sugar, salt and mustard thoroughly.
3. Combine with vinegar and egg yolks in double boiler.
4. Cook until thick, stirring constantly.
5. Remove from heat, add gelatin and stir until dissolved.
6. Add horseradish.
7. Chill until mixture begins to thicken.
8. Add salmon and celery and fold in cream.
9. Place olive slices and pimiento strips in bottom of oiled fish mold.
10. Turn mixture into mold. Chill until firm.
11. Unmold onto platter. Garnish with watercress.

Molded Crab Salad

8 TO 10
SERVINGS

1 cup water
1 package (3 ounces) lemon-
flavored gelatin
½ cup diced green pepper
½ cup diced onion
½ cup diced celery
1 cup cooked crab meat
¾ cup condensed tomato
soup
3 ounces cream cheese,
softened

1. In a 2-cup glass measure, heat water and gelatin 2 to 3 minutes, until mixture boils, stirring once halfway through cooking time. Cool about 20 minutes.
2. Add green pepper, onion, celery, and crab meat; stir to blend. Pour into oiled mold and refrigerate about 2 hours, until firm.
4. Unmold to serve.

Cinnamon Waldorf Molds

6 TO 8
SERVINGS

⅓ cup red cinnamon candies
3 cups water
2 packages (3 ounces each)
cherry-flavored gelatin
1 tablespoon lemon juice
2 cups chopped celery
2 cups chopped unpared red
apples
1 cup miniature
marshmallows
½ cup chopped walnuts
Lettuce

1. Heat cinnamon candies and water to boiling in a saucepan. Remove from heat and add gelatin and lemon juice; stir until gelatin and candies are dissolved.
2. Chill until slightly thickened.
3. Mix in celery, apples, marshmallows, and walnuts. Spoon into 6 to 8 individual fancy molds or turn into a 1½-quart mold. Chill until firm.
4. Unmold onto lettuce.

Piquant Perfection Salad

1½ cups boiling water
1 package (6 ounces) lemon-
flavored gelatin
1 can (8 ounces) crushed
pineapple in juice
Water
1 can or bottle (12 ounces)
beer
3 medium carrots, shredded
(about 1½ cups)
½ small head cabbage, finely
shredded (about 3 cups)

Piquant Perfection Salad

1. Pour boiling water over gelatin; stir until dissolved.
2. Drain pineapple, thoroughly pressing out and reserving juice. Add enough water to juice to measure ¾ cup.
3. Add juice and beer to gelatin. Chill until partially thickened.
4. Stir in carrots, cabbage, and pineapple. Turn into a shallow pan or oiled 6½-cup ring mold or any 1½-quart mold. Chill until set.
5. Dip mold briefly in hot water; invert on a serving platter.
6. Serve with a dressing of **1 cup mayonnaise** blended with **2 tablespoons beer.**
12 HALF-CUP SERVINGS

Peach Wine Mold

Peach Wine Mold

ABOUT
8 SERVINGS

1 can (29 ounces) sliced
  peaches
1 package (6 ounces) lemon-
  flavored gelatin
1½ cups boiling water
1 cup white wine
⅓ cup sliced celery
⅓ cup slivered blanched
  almonds
Curly endive

1. Drain peaches thoroughly reserving 1¼ cups syrup. Reserve and refrigerate about 8 peach slices for garnish. Cut remaining peaches into pieces; set aside.
2. Pour gelatin into a bowl, add boiling water, and stir until gelatin is dissolved. Stir in reserved syrup and wine. Chill until partially set.
3. Mix peaches, celery, and almonds into gelatin. Turn into a 1½-quart fancy mold. Chill until firm.
4. Unmold salad onto a serving plate. Garnish with curly endive and reserved peach slices.

Molded Fruit Salad

6 TO 8
SERVINGS

⅔ cup pineapple juice
⅓ cup water
1 package (3 ounces) lemon-
  flavored gelatin
1 cup well-drained canned
  pineapple chunks
¼ cup lemon juice
¼ cup chopped walnuts
2 tablespoons chopped
  maraschino cherries

1. In a 2-cup glass measure, combine pineapple juice and water and heat to boiling, about 2½ to 3 minutes.
2. Dissolve gelatin in hot mixture. Chill until thickened and syrupy, about 20 minutes.
3. Combine pineapple chunks, lemon juice, walnuts, cherries, salt, and apple in mixing bowl. Fold in whipped cream and thickened gelatin mixture.
4. Chill about 2 hours until firm.

Seafoam Salad

4 OR 5
SERVINGS

1 package (3 ounces) lime-
  flavored gelatin
¾ cup boiling water
Dash salt
1 cup diced cucumber,
  drained
2 tablespoons lemon juice
1 teaspoon minced onion
1 cup dairy sour cream

1. In a 2-cup glass measure, combine gelatin and water. Heat until boiling, about 1½ to 2 minutes, stirring halfway through cooking time. Add salt and chill until slightly thickened, about 20 minutes.
2. Stir in cucumber, lemon juice, and onion. Fold in sour cream until marbled effect is produced.
3. Pour into mold. Chill.
4. Unmold when ready to serve.

Fruit-Filled Gelatin Salad

ABOUT
12 SERVINGS

1 cup mayonnaise
1½ tablespoons lemon juice
¼ cup chilled whipping cream
2½ tablespoons sifted
   confectioners' sugar
1 20-oz. can crushed pineapple
   (about 1½ cups drained)
1 16-oz. can sliced peaches
   (about 1¼ cups, drained)
2 medium-size oranges
Orange juice (enough to make
   2 cups liquid)
2 3-oz. pkgs. cherry-flavored
   gelatin
2 cups very hot water
¼ cup lemon juice

1. For Lemon Mayonnaise – Set a bowl and beater in refrigerator to chill.
2. Set out mayonnaise.
3. Beat in 1½ tablespoons lemon juice.
4. Using the chilled bowl and beater, beat whipping cream until it is of medium consistency (piles softly).
5. With final few strokes, beat or blend in confectioners' sugar.
6. Fold into mayonnaise mixture.
7. For Salad – Drain, reserving syrup in a 2-cup measuring cup for liquids, contents of can crushed pineapple and can sliced peaches.
8. Rinse oranges. With a sharp knife, cut away peel and white membrane. Remove sections by cutting on either side of dividing membranes; remove, section by section, over the measuring cup to collect juice.
9. Put fruit into a bowl, cover, and put in refrigerator until ready to use.
10. Add orange juice to reserved syrup.
11. Empty gelatin into a large bowl.
12. Add water stirring constantly.
13. Stir until gelatin is completely dissolved; blend in the reserved fruit and lemon juice.
14. Chill in refrigerator or in pan of ice and water until gelatin mixture is slightly thicker than consistency of thick, unbeaten egg white. (If mixture is placed over ice and water, stir frequently; if it is placed in the refrigerator, stir occasionally.)
15. Lightly oil a 1½-qt. fancy mold with salad or cooking oil (not olive oil). Set it aside to drain.
16. When gelatin is of desired consistency, stir in the pineapple, peaches, and orange sections. Turn mixture into prepared mold. Place in refrigerator to chill until firm.
17. Unmold onto chilled serving platter. Serve with the Lemon Mayonnaise.

Jewel Mold: Follow recipe for Fruit-Filled Gelatin Salad. Omit fruit. Substitute 2 cups **orange juice** for the 2 cups fruit syrup. Pour mixture into a prepared 1-qt. fancy mold and chill until firm.
ABOUT 8 SERVINGS

Fruit Salads

Party Fruit Salad

8 TO 10 SERVINGS

1 can (20 ounces) pineapple chunks, drained, reserving 2 tablespoons juice
1 can (17 ounces) Royal Ann cherries, pitted and drained
1 can (11 ounces) mandarin oranges, drained
2 cups seedless grapes
1 large apple, pared, cored, and diced
2 cups miniature marshmallows
2 eggs
2 tablespoons sugar
2 tablespoons pineapple juice
2 tablespoons brandy or rosé wine
½ teaspoon dry mustard
½ cup dairy sour cream

1. In a large salad bowl, combine pineapple chunks, cherries, orange sections, grapes, apple, and marshmallows. Chill until serving time.
2. In a 2-cup glass measure, combine eggs, sugar, pineapple juice, brandy, and dry mustard. Stir with wire whip to blend well. cook 2 to 3 minutes, stirring every 30 seconds, until mixture thickens and is light. Cool.
3. Drain excess liquid from fruit. Fold cooled dressings and sour cream into fruit until evenly blended. Chill until serving time.

Chef's Fruit Salad

ABOUT 6 SERVINGS

Cinnamon-Buttered Raisins:
1 tablespoon butter or margarine, melted
½ cup dark raisins
½ cup golden raisins
½ teaspoon ground cinnamon

Salad:
Salad greens
1 quart shredded salad greens
6 cups mixed fruit
Creamy Lemon Celery-Seed Dressing or Celery-Seed Salad Dressing
1½ cups Swiss cheese strips
1½ cups cooked ham or turkey strips

1. For Cinnamon-Buttered Raisins, melt butter in a skillet. Mix in raisins and cinnamon. Set over low heat 5 minutes, stirring frequently. Cool.
2. Line a salad bowl with salad greens. Add shredded greens.
3. Arrange fruit in bowl. Spoon some of the desired dressing over all. Top with cheese and ham strips alternated with Cinnamon-Buttered Raisins. Serve with remaining dressing.

Creamy Lemon Celery-Seed Dressing; Blend thoroughly 1½ cups mayonnaise, ¼ cup unsweetened pineapple juice, 1 teaspoon grated lemon peel, 1 tablespoon lemon juice, ½ teaspoon celery seed, and few drops Tabasco. Cover and refrigerate at least 1 hour to blend flavors. ABOUT 1½ CUPS DRESSING

Celery-Seed Salad Dressing: Combine in a small bowl ¼ cup sugar, ⅓ cup light corn syrup, ¼ cup cider vinegar, 1½ to 2 teaspoons celery seed, 1 teaspoon dry mustard, 1 teaspoon salt, few grains white pepper, and 1 teaspoon grated onion. Beat with a rotary beater until mixture is thoroughly blended. Add 1 cup salad oil very gradually, beating constantly. Continue beating until mixture thickens. Cover and chill thoroughly. Shake before serving. 2 CUPS DRESSING

Marinated Fruit Salad

SERVES 8

2 apples
3 pears
3 peaches
1 pineapple
Confectioners sugar
¼ cup rum or Cointreau

1. Pare, core and slice apples and pears. Halve, pit, peel and slice peaches. Cut pineapple into chunks.
2. Place fruit in a bowl and sprinkle with confectioners sugar to taste. Sprinkle with rum or Cointreau.
3. Cover the bowl tightly and chill for at least 6 hours so the sugar draws out fruit juices.

Rooster's Bill

4 TO 6
SERVINGS

1 medium jícama*
1 large orange
¼ cup chopped onion
Juice of 1 lemon
1 teaspoon salt
1 teaspoon chili powder
½ teaspoon oregano,
   crumbled

1. Wash, pare, and chop jícama into ½-inch chunks.
2. Pare and section orange, reserving juice, and add to jícama; pour orange juice over fruit chunks. Add onion, lemon juice, and salt and stir until evenly mixed. Let stand at least 1 hour in refrigerator before serving.
3. When ready to serve, sprinkle with chili powder and oregano.

*3 large tart crisp apples may be substituted for jícama.

Northwest Fruit Slaw

Northwest Fruit Slaw

1 can (16 ounces) light sweet
   cherries
1 can (16 ounces) dark sweet
   cherries
3 fresh Anjou, Bosc, or
   Comice pears
2 cups finely shredded
   cabbage
Creamy Fruit Mayonnaise
   (page 78)
Lettuce

1. Drain cherries and remove pits. Reserve a few cherries for garnish. Core and dice 1 pear. Core and slice remaining pears into wedges for garnish.
2. Combine cabbage, cherries, and diced pear. Add Creamy Fruit Mayonnaise and toss lightly to coat fruit and cabbage.
3. Line a serving bowl with lettuce and spoon in salad. Garnish with pear wedges and reserved cherries.
ABOUT 8 SERVINGS

Marinated Fruit Salad

Fruit Salad with Ice Cream Topping

SERVES 8

4 pears, cored
1 large melon wedge
1 can Mandarin orange
  wedges
½ can pineapple
Green grapes (optional)
2 pints vanilla ice cream
1 cup fresh orange juice
Orange rind

1. Cut the pears and melon wedge in pieces and mix with the canned fruits.
2. Pour in a little of the syrup from the cans. Cover and let salad stand in refrigerator until chilled.
3. Divide the ice cream into 8 dishes.
4. Distribute fruit on top of ice cream.
5. Just before serving, pour on the fresh orange juice. Sprinkle with finely slivered orange rind or coconut.

Waldorf Salad

ABOUT
4 SERVINGS

2 medium-size red apples
  (about 2 cups, diced)
1 cup chopped celery
½ cup (about 2 oz.) chopped
  walnuts
¼ teaspoon salt
¼ cup mayonnaise

1. Wash apples, quarter, core and dice.
2. Combine with celery and walnuts.
3. Sprinkle with salt.
4. Add mayonnaise and toss lightly.
5. Chill in refrigerator until ready to serve.
6. Serve in crisp lettuce cups. If desired, sprinkle with paprika or cinnamon.

California Fruit Plate

4 SERVINGS

2 cups low-fat cottage cheese
8 fresh figs, cut in quarters
2 cups fresh raspberries
2 tablespoons honey
4 lemon wedges

1. Place ½ cup cottage cheese on each of 4 salad plates.
2. Surround cottage cheese with 8 quarters of fig; sprinkle raspberries over figs.
3. Drizzle honey over fruit and cottage cheese. Squeeze lemon over all.

Overnight Coconut Fruit Salad

ABOUT
6 SERVINGS

1 11-oz. can mandarin oranges
  (about 1 cup, drained)
1 8¼-oz. can crushed pineapple
  (about ¾ cup, drained)
1 cup orange sections
8 (2 oz.) marshmallows
1 cup (about 4 oz.) moist
  shredded coconut, cut
1 cup thick sour cream
2 tablespoons sugar

1. Drain, reserving syrup for use in other food preparation, contents of can of mandarin oranges and can of crushed pineapple.
2. Prepare and section enough oranges to yield 1 cup orange sections.
3. Cut marshmallows into quarters.
4. Put the mandarin oranges, pineapple, orange sections and marshmallows into a large bowl with the moist shredded coconut.
5. Mix together sour cream and sugar.
6. Pour over the fruit mixture and toss lightly to mix thoroughly. Cover; chill in refrigerator overnight.
7. To serve, spoon portions of salad onto chilled serving plates lined with crisp salad greens. Garnish with mint sprigs.

Fruit Salad with Ice Cream Topping

Sparkling Peach Salad

16 SERVINGS

6 cups ginger ale
3 envelopes unflavored gelatin
2 cans (17 ounces each) sliced
  peaches, drained
2 tablespoons finely chopped
  crystallized ginger

1. Pour 1 cup of ginger ale into a small saucepan. Sprinkle gelatin over it. Stir over low heat until gelatin is dissolved. Stir gelatin into remaining ginger ale.
2. Chill gelatin until slightly thicker than consistency of thick unbeaten egg white. Mix in peaches and ginger. Turn into a 9-inch square pan and chill until firm. Cut into squares.

Christmas Eve Salad

8 TO 10
SERVINGS

1 cup diced cooked beets
1 cup diced tart apple, not
  peeled
1 cup orange sections
1 cup sliced bananas
1 cup diced pineapple (fresh
  or canned)
Juice of 1 lime
Oil and Vinegar Dressing
Shredded lettuce
½ cup chopped peanuts
Seeds from 1 pomegranate

1. Drain beets well. Combine beets, apple, oranges, bananas, and pineapple. Refrigerate until ready to serve.
2. Add lime juice to beet-fruit mixture. Add desired amount of dressing and toss until evenly mixed and coated with dressing.
3. To serve, make a bed of shredded lettuce in salad bowl. Mound salad on top. Sprinkle with peanuts and pomegranate seeds.

Beer-Curried Fruit

7 CUPS

½ cup packed brown sugar
1 tablespoon cornstarch
2 to 3 teaspoons curry
  powder
¾ cup beer
¼ cup butter or margarine
1 tablespoon grated orange
  peel
1 can (30 ounces) cling peach
  slices, drained
1 can (29 ounces) cling pear
  halves or slices, drained
2 cans (11 ounces each) mandarin oranges, drained
2 bananas, thinly sliced

1. In a large saucepan, combine sugar, cornstarch, and curry powder. Stir in beer. Cook, stirring constantly, until thickened and clear.
2. Add butter and orange peel; stir until melted.
3. Add peaches, pears, and mandarin oranges. (If using pear halves, cut into slices.) Cover and simmer about 10 minutes. Stir in bananas.
4. Turn into a serving dish, chafing dish, or warming dish. Sprinkle with **flaked coconut.**

Empress Salad

Escarole
Watermelon chunks
Pear cubes (unpared)
Cucumber cubes (pared)
French Dressing (page 74; use
  lemon juice)

1. Wash and thoroughly chill salad ingredients before preparing salad. Set out a salad bowl.
2. Tear escarole into pieces.
3. Prepare watermelon chunks, pear cubes, and cucumber cubes.
4. Put the fruit and cucumber cubes into the salad bowl with the escarole. Pour on French dressing (using just enough to coat fruit and greens).
5. Toss lightly and serve immediately.

Christmas Eve Salad

Frozen Salads

Cucumber Frost

6 SERVINGS

16 (¼ lb.) marshmallows
2 medium-size (about 1½ lbs.)
    cucumbers
⅓ cup lemon juice
½ to 1 teaspoon grated onion
½ teaspoon salt
Few grains cayenne pepper
Green food coloring (about 3
    drops)
2 egg whites
1 tablespoon sugar
6 Tomato Shells (page 23)
Lettuce leaves

1. Set refrigerator control at colder operating temperature. Set a bowl in refrigerator to chill.
2. **For Cucumber Frost** *(About 1 qt.)* – Cut marshmallows into quarters and put into the top of a double boiler.
3. Place over simmering water, stirring occasionally until softened.
4. Meanwhile, rinse and pare cucumbers.
5. Cut into halves lengthwise; remove and discard seeds. Grate enough of the cucumbers to yield 2 cups pulp and juice. Drain pulp; mix lemon juice, onion, salt and cayenne pepper with the juice.
6. Add green food coloring gradually to the marshmallows, stirring over simmering water until mixture is completely blended and smooth. Add the cucumber pulp and blend well. Tint by blending in food coloring, a drop at a time.
7. Pour mixture into refrigerator tray and freeze until mushlike in consistency.
8. When mixture is mushlike, beat egg whites until frothy.
9. Add sugar and beat until rounded peaks are formed.
10. Turn the cucumber mixture into the chilled bowl and beat with rotary beater just until smooth. Add the egg white mixture and fold in thoroughly.
11. Return mixture to refrigerator tray and freeze until firm (3 to 4 hrs.).
12. **To Complete Salad** – Prepare and chill tomato shells.
13. When ready to serve, line chilled salad plates with lettuce leaves.
14. Put one tomato shell on each plate. Put a scoop of Cucumber Frost in the center of each tomato.

Nippy Cheese Freeze Salad

6 TO 8 SERVINGS

10 stuffed olives
3 oz. natural cheese food
½ cup thick sour cream
1 teaspoon lemon juice
3 drops Tabasco
Lettuce
Curly endive
Romaine
Watercress
1 clove garlic, cut into halves

1. **For Nippy Cheese Freeze** – Set refrigerator control at colder operating temperature.
2. Chop olives and set aside.
3. Put cheese food into a small bowl and mash with a fork.
4. Add sour cream gradually, blending until mixture is smooth.
5. Blend in the chopped olives, lemon juice and Tabasco.
6. Turn mixture into a 1-qt. refrigerator tray. Put into freezing compartment of refrigerator and freeze until mixture is firm.
7. **For Tossed Salad** – Rinse lettuce, curly endive, romaine and watercress, discarding bruised leaves, drain and dry thoroughly.
8. Using as much of each green as desired, tear into pieces enough greens to yield about 2 qts. Put into a large plastic bag or vegetable freshener. Chill in refrigerator at least 1 hr.

9. When ready to serve, rub a salad bowl with cut surface of garlic.
10. Cut the frozen cheese mixture into small cubes.
11. Put the chilled greens into the salad bowl and toss lightly with **French dressing.** Add the cheese cubes and toss just enough to distribute the cubes evenly throughout the greens.
12. Serve immediately.

Garlic Cottage-Cheese Freeze: Follow recipe for Nippy Cheese Freeze Salad. Use two refrigerator trays. Substitute **ripe olives** for stuffed olives and 2 cups sieved **cream-style cottage cheese** for cheese food. Blend in 1 clove **garlic** crushed in garlic press or minced.

Greengage Plum Salad

6 TO 8
SERVINGS

2½ cups canned greengage
  plums and syrup (about 2¼
  cups, sieved)
1 cup chopped celery
½ cup (about 2 oz.) chopped
  walnuts

1. Set refrigerator control at colder operating temperature.
2. Cut plums into halves, remove and discard pits, and force plums and syrup through a sieve or food mill.
3. Prepare and mix in celery and walnuts.
4. Turn into a refrigerator tray.
5. Put into freezing compartment of refrigerator and freeze until mixture is firm (about 4 hrs.), stirring 2 or 3 times.

Pear and Frozen Cheese Salad

8 SERVINGS

4 ounces Roquefort or blue
  cheese (1 cup, crumbled)
½ cup chopped celery
3 ounces (1 package) cream
  cheese
¼ cup mayonnaise
1 tablespoon lemon juice
¼ teaspoon salt
⅛ teaspoon pepper
½ cup chilled whipping
  cream
4 chilled, ripe Bartlett pears
Lemon juice
Curly endive, watercress, or
  other salad greens
French dressing

1. Crumble Roquefort or blue cheese and set aside.
2. Prepare celery and set aside.
3. Beat cream cheese until fluffy.
4. Mix in mayonnaise and lemon juice, and a mixture of salt and pepper, stirring until thoroughly blended after each addition.
5. Stir in the crumbled cheese and chopped celery. Set mixture aside.
6. Using a chilled bowl and beater, beat whipping cream until cream is of medium consistency (piles softly).
7. Gently fold into cheese mixture. Turn into a chilled refrigerator tray. Put into freezing compartment of refrigerator and freeze until cheese mixture is firm.
8. When ready to serve, cut frozen cheese into 1-inch cubes.
9. *For Bartlett Pear Salad* – Rinse well, cut into halves and core Bartlett pears.
10. Brush cut sides of pears with lemon juice.
11. Place salad greens on each of 8 chilled salad plates.
12. Put one pear half, cut side up, on each plate. Place two or three frozen Roquefort or blue cheese cubes in hollow of each pear half. Or arrange greens, pear halves and cheese cubes on a large chilled serving plate.
13. Serve immediately with French dressing.

Frozen Fruit Salad

8 TO 10
SERVINGS

½ cup (about 3 oz.) almonds
1 20-oz. can crushed pineapple
(about 1¾ cups, drained)
½ cup maraschino cherries
½ cup (about 3 oz.) pitted dates
24 (6 oz.) marshmallows
8 oz. cream cheese, softened
¼ cup mayonnaise
1 cup chilled whipping cream

1. Set refrigerator control at colder operating temperature. Set a bowl and rotary beater in refrigerator to chill. Set out a 1½-qt. mold or large refrigerator tray.
2. Blanch, toast, and salt almonds.
3. Chop coarsely and set aside.
4. Set out can of crushed pineapple to drain, reserving syrup.
5. Cut maraschino cherries into quarters and set aside on absorbent paper to drain. (To avoid a pink tint in the mixture, drain cherries thoroughly.)
6. Cut dates into slivers and set aside.
7. Cut marshmallows into eighths and set aside.
8. Beat until well blended 3 tablespoons of the reserved pineapple syrup and cream cheese.
9. Mix in mayonnaise.
10. Gently mix in nuts, fruits and marshmallows.
11. Using the chilled bowl and beater, beat chilled whipping cream until cream is of medium consistency.
12. Lightly spread over cheese mixture and fold together. Turn into mold or refrigerator tray. Freeze until firm (about 4 hrs.).
13. Unmold onto chilled serving plate and garnish base with **fruit** and sprigs of **mint** or **watercress.** Or serve slices or wedges of the salad on chilled individual salad plates.
14. Serve with **pineapple salad dressing** (page 78).

Frozen Tropical Salad: Follow recipe for Frozen Fruit Salad. Substitute **pecans** for almonds and ¾ cup diced **banana** for the dates.

Note: If desired, turn salad mixture into 2 29-oz. cans or 3 16-oz. cans, washed and drained. Freeze until firm.

Frozen Peppermint Dessert Salad

ABOUT
20 SERVINGS

1 20-oz. can crushed pineapple
(about 2½ cups)
1 3-oz. pkg.
strawberry-flavored gelatin
1 pkg. (10½ oz.) miniature
marshmallows
¼ cup (about 2 oz.) cinnamon
candies
2 cups chilled whipping cream
¼ lb. soft butter mints, crushed

1. Put pineapple, gelatin and marshmallows into a large bowl.
2. Add cinnamon candies.
3. Mix well, cover and put into refrigerator to chill overnight.
4. Meanwhile, set refrigerator control at colder operating temperature. Set a bowl and rotary beater in refrigerator to chill.
5. Using the chilled bowl and beater, beat whipping cream (one cup at a time) until cream is of medium consistency (piles softly).
6. Fold whipped cream into pineapple mixture with butter mints.
7. Turn into refrigerator trays or a 10-in. tubed pan. Freeze until firm.

Note: The strawberry-flavored gelatin is used for flavor and color rather than for gelling the mixture.

Stocks and Dressings

Vinaigrette Dressing

ABOUT
1/2 CUP

1 tablespoon fresh lemon
  juice
1 tablespoon olive or
  vegetable oil
1/4 cup Chicken Stock (page
  76)
2 teaspoons snipped parsley
1 teaspoon snipped fresh or
  1/2 teaspoon dried basil
  leaves
2 teaspoons distilled white
  vinegar
1 teaspoon Dijon mustard
1 small garlic clove, minced
1/8 teaspoon salt
Freshly ground white pepper

Measure all ingredients into a jar with a tight cover; shake vigorously. Refrigerate dressing until chilled. Shake before serving.

Russian Dressing

MAKES
1 3/4 CUPS

1 cup salad oil
1/2 cup catchup
1/3 cup vinegar
2 tablespoons sugar
1 teaspoon salt
1/2 teaspoon grated onion

1. Combine all ingredients in the order listed and beat until thoroughly blended.

Italian Dressing

ABOUT
1 1/2 CUP
DRESSING

6 tablespoons olive oil
3 tablespoons wine vinegar
1 clove garlic, crushed in a
  garlic press
1/4 teaspoon salt
1/8 teaspoon pepper

1. Place all ingredients in a screw-top jar, shake well, and chill.
2. Just before serving, beat or shake thoroughly.

Anchovy Dressing: Follow recipe for Italian Dressing. Add **1 teaspoon prepared mustard** and **2 finely chopped anchovy fillets** to jar before shaking.

Low-Fat Yogurt

ABOUT
1 QUART

1 quart 2% milk
¼ cup instant nonfat
  dry-milk
2 tablespoons low-fat natural
  yogurt

1. Mix milk and dry-milk solids in a medium saucepan. Heat to scalding (150°F); cool to 110°F. Stir in yogurt.
2. Transfer mixture to a glass or crockery bowl. Cover with plastic wrap; wrap bowl securely in a heavy bath towel. Set in warm place (100° to 125°F)* for 4 to 6 hours, until yogurt has formed.
3. Place several layers of paper toweling directly on yogurt; refrigerate covered until cold.

*A gas oven with a pilot light will be about 125°F; however, use an oven thermometer, as temperature is very important. Turn an electric oven to as warm a setting as necessary to maintain temperature.
  Excess liquid and a coarse texture will result if temperature is too high. Liquid can be drained with a nylon baster. Blend yogurt in a food processor or blender to restore texture.

Note: This recipe can be made using skim or reconstituted dry milk, although the product will not be as rich.
  Purchased low-fat natural yogurt can be substituted in any recipe.

Green Goddess Salad Dressing

ABOUT
2½ CUPS
DRESSING

1 cup mayonnaise
½ cup thick sour cream
3 tablespoons tarragon
  vinegar
1 tablespoon lemon juice
⅓ cup finely chopped
  parsley
3 tablespoons finely chopped
  onion
3 tablespoons mashed
  anchovy fillets
1 tablespoon chopped chives
2 teaspoons chopped capers
1 clove garlic, crushed in a
  garlic press or minced
⅛ teaspoon salt
⅛ teaspoon pepper

1. Blend all ingredients thoroughly.
2. Cover bowl tightly and chill in refrigerator 3 to 4 hours.
3. Serve on Green Goddess Salad.

French Dressing Antillaise for Salads

½ cup olive oil
1 teaspoon salt
½ teaspoon freshly ground
  pepper
2 garlic cloves
Tarragon, dill, or oregano to
  taste
5 parsley sprigs
2 scallions or green onions,
  finely chopped
1 tablespoon wine vinegar

1. Pour oil into a salad bowl; add remaining ingredients. With a pestle or wooden spoon, rub herbs against the side of the bowl and mix with oil.
2. For salad, marinate your choice of **celery pieces, chickpeas, onion slices, cherry tomatoes, sliced mushrooms, sliced cooked beets,** or **beans** (never more than two) in dressing for at least 1 hour before serving.
3. To serve, toss chilled **salad greens** with marinated vegetables.

Salad with French Dressing Antillaise

French Dressing

ABOUT
1 CUP DRESSING

¾ cup salad oil or olive oil
¼ cup lemon juice or cider vinegar
1 tablespoon sugar
¾ teaspoon salt
¼ teaspoon paprika
¼ teaspoon dry mustard
¼ teaspoon pepper

1. Combine in a screw-top jar salad or olive oil, lemon juice or cider vinegar, sugar, salt, paprika, dry mustard and pepper.
2. Cover jar tightly and shake vigorously to blend well. Store in covered container in refrigerator.
3. Shake well before using.

Anchovy French Dressing: Follow recipe for French Dressing. Use lemon juice. Omit salt and add 4 minced **anchovy fillets.** Shake well.

Lorenzo French Dressing: Follow recipe for French Dressing. Add ¼ cup finely chopped **watercress** and 2 tablespoons **chili sauce.** Shake well.

Olive French Dressing: Follow recipe for French Dressing. Add ½ cup chopped **stuffed olives** and shake well.

Tangy French Dressing: Follow recipe for French Dressing. Add 3 to 4 tablespoons **prepared horseradish** and shake well.

Curried French Dressing: Follow recipe for French Dressing. Add ¼ teaspoon **curry powder** and shake well.

Fruit Juice French Dressing: Follow recipe for French Dressing. Substitute **orange** or **pineapple juice** for the lemon juice or vinegar, or use 2 tablespoons of each fruit juice.

Creamy French Dressing: Follow recipe for French Dressing. Add ¼ cup **thick sour cream** and blend well.

Garlic French Dressing: Cut into halves 1 clove **garlic;** add to completed dressing. Chill dressing about 12 hours before using to allow flavors to blend. Remove garlic before serving or when flavor of dressing is sufficiently strong.

Roquefort French Dressing: Follow recipe for French Dressing. Blend together until smooth 3 ounces (about ¾ cup) crumbled **Roquefort cheese** and 2 teaspoons **water.** Add dressing slowly to cheese, blending after each addition.

Honey-Lime French Dressing: Follow recipe for French Dressing. Substitute **lime juice** for the lemon juice or vinegar. Blend in ½ cup **honey** and ¼ teaspoon grated **lime peel.**

Vinaigrette French Dressing: Follow recipe for French Dressing. Add 2 tablespoons finely chopped **dill pickle,** 1 tablespoon chopped **chives,** and **1 hard-cooked egg** chopped. Shake well.

Italian Dressing: Follow recipe for French Dressing. Use olive oil. Omit lemon juice or vinegar and add 6 tablespoons wine vinegar. Reduce salt to ½ teaspoon. Omit sugar, paprika and dry mustard. Shake well.

Tomato Soup French Dressing: Follow recipe for French Dressing. Add ⅔ cup (about one-half 10½-to 11 ounce can) **condensed tomato soup,** 1 tablespoon chopped **onion** and ½ teaspoon **marjoram.** Shake well.

Honey French Dressing: Follow recipe for French Dressing. Use lemon juice. Blend in ½ cup **honey** and ¼ teaspoon grated **lemon peel.** For added flavor, add ½ teaspoon **celery seed** and shake well.

Chiffonade French Dressing: Follow recipe for French Dressing. Add 1 **hard-cooked egg,** chopped, 2 tablespoons finely chopped **ripe olives,** and 4 teaspoons finely chopped **parsley.** Shake well.

Tarragon French Dressing: Follow recipe for French Dressing. Use olive oil. Substitute **tarragon vinegar** for lemon juice or cider vinegar. Decrease sugar to 1 teaspoon. Add 1 clove **garlic,** cut into halves, ¼ teaspoon **Worcestershire sauce** and ⅛ teaspoon **thyme.** Shake well.

Cooked Salad Dressing

ABOUT
1½ CUPS
SALAD DRESSING

¼ cup sugar
1 tablespoon all-purpose flour
½ teaspoon dry mustard
½ teaspoon salt
⅛ teaspoon pepper
1 cup water
¼ cup cider vinegar
4 egg yolks, slightly beaten
2 tablespoons butter

1. Mix sugar, flour, dry mustard, salt and pepper thoroughly in the top of a double boiler.
2. Blend water in gradually.
3. Set over direct heat. Stirring gently and constantly, bring mixture to boiling. Cook 1 to 2 min. longer. Add and stir in vinegar.
4. Vigorously stir about 3 tablespoons of the hot mixture into egg yolks.
5. Immediately blend into mixture in top of double boiler. Place over simmering water and cook 3 to 5 min., stirring slowly to keep mixture cooking evenly. Remove from heat and stir in butter.
6. Cool; store in covered container in refrigerator. Before using, thin to desired consistency with cream, fruit juice or cider vinegar.

Dressing for Overnight Fruit Salad: Follow recipe for Cooked Salad Dressing. Use 2 tablespoons **sugar,** 2 tablespoons **cider vinegar** and 2 tablespoons **pineapple syrup.** Bring mixture only to boiling. Substitute 3 **egg yolks** and 1 tablespoon **butter.** When dressing is cooled, beat 1 cup chilled **whipping cream** until it is of medium consistency (piles softly). Fold the cooked dressing into the whipped cream.
ABOUT 2 CUPS DRESSING

Blue Cheese Sour Cream Dressing

ABOUT
1½ CUPS
DRESSING

1 package blue cheese salad dressing mix
1 package (3 ounces) cream cheese, softened
1 cup sour cream

1. Prepare salad dressing following package directions.
2. Blend dressing with cream cheese in a bowl. Stir in sour cream until dressing is of desired consistency.
3. Serve dressing with **fruit and vegetable salad.**

Garlic Mayonnaise

ABOUT
1½ CUPS

4 garlic cloves, crushed in a garlic press
¼ teaspoon salt
2 egg yolks
Olive oil (about 1 cup)
Juice of ½ lemon, or more to taste
Salt and white pepper

1. Combine garlic, salt, and egg yolks.
2. Slowly add oil, a drop at a time, beating vigorously until 2 to 3 tablespoons have been added. Add remaining oil in a steady stream, beating constantly.
3. Add lemon juice, beating well. Season with salt and pepper.

Chicken Stock

3 TO 3½
QUARTS

5 pounds chicken backs and wings, or stewing chicken, cut up
3 carrots, cut in 2-inch pieces
2 medium yellow onions, quartered
1 stalk celery, cut in 2-inch pieces
2 teaspoons salt
Bouquet garni:
 ¾ teaspoon dried thyme leaves
 ¾ teaspoon dried rosemary leaves
 1 bay leaf
 4 sprigs parsley
 2 whole cloves
Water

1. Place chicken, vegetables, salt, and bouquet garni in an 8-quart Dutch oven. Pour in water to cover (about 4 quarts). Simmer covered 2 to 2½ hours.
2. Strain stock through a double thickness of cheesecloth into a storage container. Taste for seasoning. If more concentrated flavor is desired, return stock to saucepan and simmer 20 to 30 minutes, or dissolve 1 to 2 teaspoons instant chicken bouillon in the stock.
3. Store covered in refrigerator or freezer. Remove solidified fat from top of stock before using.

Note: Refrigerated stock is perishable. If not used within several days, heat to boiling, cool, and refrigerate or freeze to prevent spoilage. Stock can be kept frozen up to 4 months.

Court Bouillon for Fish and Shellfish

ABOUT
1 QUART

1 onion
1 leek
1 carrot
3 celery stalks
5 parsley sprigs
1 basil sprig
2 tablespoons olive oil
2 quarts boiling water
Bouquet garni
6 peppercorns, cracked
2 whole cloves
6 dried Italian pepper pods or 1 whole pink hot pepper
½ cup amber rum

1. Finely chop fresh vegetables and herbs together.
2. Heat oil in a large saucepan, add chopped mixture, and cook until lightly browned. Add boiling water, bouquet garni, peppercorns, cloves, pepper pods, and rum. Cover; boil 30 minutes. Boil uncovered to reduce volume by half.
3. Strain and cool before using.

Blue Cheese Sour Cream Dressing

Pineapple Salad Dressing

ABOUT
4 CUPS
DRESSING

1½ cups pineapple juice
½ cup sugar
1 tablespoon cornstarch
⅛ teaspoon salt
2 egg yolks, slightly beaten
2 egg whites
2 tablespoons sugar
2 tablespoons butter
¾ cup chilled whipping cream

1. Set out pineapple juice.
2. Sift together sugar, cornstarch and salt into top of a double boiler.
3. Stir in ½ cup of the pineapple juice. Stirring gently and constantly, bring mixture rapidly to boiling over direct heat and cook for 3 min. Place over simmering water. Vigorously stir about 3 tablespoons of the hot mixture into egg yolks.
4. Immediately blend into mixture in double boiler. Cook over simmering water 3 to 5 min. Stir slowly to keep mixture cooking evenly. Remove double boiler from heat.
5. Beat egg whites until frothy.
6. Add 2 tablespoons sugar gradually, beating well after each addition.
7. Beat until rounded peaks are formed. Gently blend into mixture in top of double boiler.
8. Heat the remaining 1 cup pineapple juice to lukewarm. Stirring constantly, gradually add to egg white mixture.
9. Cook over simmering water until thick and smooth, stirring constantly (about 10 min.). Add and stir butter until melted.
10. Remove from heat and set aside to cool. Set in refrigerator to chill.
11. Meanwhile, set a bowl and rotary beater in refrigerator to chill.
12. When pineapple mixture is chilled, using the chilled bowl and beater, beat whipping cream until cream is of medium consistency (piles softly).
13. Gently fold whipped cream into pineapple mixture.

Creamy Fruit Mayonnaise

ABOUT
¾ CUP

⅓ cup mayonnaise
⅓ cup sour cream
1 tablespoon honey
1 tablespoon lemon juice
1 tablespoon orange juice
¼ teaspoon salt

Combine mayonnaise, sour cream, honey, juices, and salt, blending well.

Mock Crème Fraîche

ABOUT
2 CUPS

1½ cups Neufchatel cheese
6 tablespoons Low-Fat
   Yogurt

1. Mix cheese and yogurt in a blender or food processor until smooth and fluffy. Place in small jars; cover tightly.
2. Set jars in a warm place (100° to 125°F) for 2 hours; see Note. Cool and refrigerate. Stir before using.

Note: Use an oven thermometer in making Mock Crème Fraîche, as temperature is very important. A gas oven with a pilot light will be about 125°F. Turn electric oven to as warm a setting as necessary to maintain temperature. Mock Crème Fraîche can be refrigerated up to 3 weeks.

Index

80 • INDEX